GETTING READY TO TEACH KINDERGARTEN

by Laurie DeVault, M.Ed.

Photos by Bruce Hazelton

Illustrated by Anita DuFalla

Rosalie Cochran

Kathi Wilson

Carol McHale

We warmly thank the community of the Fern Avenue School of Torrance, California, especially Mrs. Rosalie Cochran, principal; Mrs. Carol McHale and Ms. Kathi Wilson, kindergarten teachers; and students, parents, and caregivers of Mrs. McHale's and Ms. Wilson's classes. Thanks also to Ms. Melanie Wieland, Mrs. Janice Gutierrez, and Mrs. Deanna Bonach, teachers at Alta Vista Elementary School in Redondo Beach, California.

Project Manager: Barbara G. Hoffman
Editor: Johanna Otero
Book Design: Anthony D. Paular
Cover Design: Anthony D. Paular
Pre-Press Production: Daniel Willits

FS122002 Getting Ready to Teach Kindergarten
All rights reserved—Printed in the U.S.A.
23740 Hawthorne Blvd.
Torrance, CA 90505

Let us put our minds together and see what life we can make for our children.

—Tatanba Iotanko, Sitting Bull, Lakota Sioux, 1877

CHAPTER ONE: INTRODUCTIONS

I jumped at the chance to write this book for several reasons. First, because I love teaching and also because I especially love kindergarten. Every morning I drive to my little school in the country, my head full of ideas about the day ahead. As I drive past fields, farms, and forests, I may make up a song about friendship, re-think an activity, or make a mental note to spend time with a child I'm concerned about. Every day I look forward to stepping inside my classroom with its assortment of paints, blocks, and little wooden chairs. Every day is full of promise and possibilities.

Another reason that I wrote this book is that I love sharing my ideas with others. I thought about what kind of book would have helped me years ago when I was a new teacher, and used that as my guiding light throughout the writing process.

My final reason for creating this book was my belief in the importance of the child-centered education. In an era when much emphasis has been placed on skill achievement and test scores for five- and six-year-olds, I want to show you the way to nurture children's growth in all areas. My hope is that my book will move you to always keep the child at the center of everything you do.

Learning is not a race for information. It is a walk of discovery. Joyful teaching to all!

1

HOW THIS BOOK CAN HELP YOU

There you are, like thousands of teachers before you, standing in the middle of your new classroom. Perhaps it's summer, and chairs and tables are stacked in a corner while the carpet waits to be cleaned. The walls may be bare and begging for a new coat of paint. Your eyes scan the shelves, searching for games, blocks, and bottles of paint. Depending on the school, you may rejoice over the bountiful supplies and cheerful surroundings or despair over the worn furniture and dearth of materials.

In either case, you stand alone in that room, trying to envision how it will look on opening day when about two dozen (more or less) kindergartners cross the threshold to meet you, their teacher. You sigh, shake your head, and wonder how on earth you will ever be ready!

Well, this book is designed to help you get ready for not only the Big Day, but also for the rest of the year. Even if the scenario above differs from your own situation, you must think about who your students are, what you are going to teach them, and how you are going to teach them.

This book includes ideas for a variety of activities that promote all areas of development. Topics include self-esteem, computers, literacy skill development, classroom management, and helping students with special needs.

So, take a deep breath and remember to smile. You're about to enter the wonderful and dynamic world of kindergarten!

WELCOME TO KINDERGARTEN!

What is kindergarten? Just as no two children are alike, no two kindergartens are alike. They vary in many ways, such as by length (ranging from half-day to full) and by type of school (private or public). There are schools that follow a particular approach, such as Montessori or Waldorf schools. There are urban, suburban, and rural kindergartens, some well-funded and others struggling to meet the needs of their students. Many classrooms have children from diverse cultural and racial groups while others are quite homogeneous. Some kindergartens are combined with first grades or have some other type of multi-age grouping.

There are some kindergarten classrooms where you will find rows of desks with children coloring on worksheets. In others you will see children working in structured learning centers on such specific tasks as making patterns with colored cubes, cutting shapes out of clay, and tracing letters with alphabet stencils. And, in some kindergartens you will find children exploring a wide variety of materials and directing their own learning. There are both major and subtle differences among these kindergartens. Kindergartens vary according to each teacher's goals for his or her students. Teachers also have differing views about what roles they should play in the lives of their students.

Despite these differences, most kindergarten teachers will agree that kindergarten is where children:

- gain a greater sense of autonomy than in preschool

- learn to work and play cooperatively with others

- develop a positive attitude toward school

- are encouraged to see themselves as competent learners

- participate in formal instructional activities.

> **All I ever really needed to know, I learned in kindergarten.**
>
> —Robert Fulgham, Kansas City Times

For some children, kindergarten is the very first experience being away from home. For others, it is a continuation of a preschool or day-care experience that may have begun as early as infancy. For most, it is the first introduction to "real" school, and as such is a pivotal year in their lives. As their teacher, much of the responsibility for ensuring a successful year is in your hands. It is a tremendous responsibility, but one that should bring you immeasurable joy and satisfaction!

MEET YOUR KINDERGARTNER

As a teacher new to kindergarten, it is important to know who is going to walk through that door on the first day of school. If you have a fairly solid grasp of early childhood development, and have experience working (or living) with five-year-olds, you have a general picture of who to expect on that first day of school. If you feel you need to learn more about how children learn, excellent resources are available to educators, including the works of Arnold Gesell, Jean Piaget, Erik Erikson, Lev Vygotsky, and others.

Kindergarten students may range in age from four-and-a-half to six-and-a-half. Although children grow and develop at different rates and have individual differences influenced by their environment and culture, you can have some general expectations about who your students will be. Most kindergarten teachers notice a change in their students as the school year progresses. At age six, many children begin a major change in their cognitive development. They begin to think logically, understand cause and effect, and see another's point of view.

The range of characteristics includes:

- cooperative and want to be "good"
- happy outlook on life
- accepting rules and authority
- wanting to please you and other significant adults
- literal and succinct
- seeing another person's point of view with difficulty
- unable to think logically
- active and able to inhibit behavior
- having fixed ocular vision, making reading sentences of text difficult
- learning best through active play
- able to sit for a story or task for 20 minutes
- needing frequent physical activity
- enjoying structured games and dramatic play
- emotional, and perhaps uncomfortable with the strength of their emotions
- testing limits, with possibly some oppositional behavior
- valuing friendship
- periods of high activity alternating with fatigue

- learning sportsmanship

- exploring different roles in group activities (leading, directing, and following)

- enjoying surprises and jokes

- preferring to stand while working

- occasionally confused visually and auditorally (reversals are common)

- developing gross and fine motor skills

- eager to try new tasks

- viewing process as more important than a finished product

The best way to learn about your students is to pay attention to them. Observe them, listen to them, and talk with them. They will be your best guides for helping you decide how and what you need to teach!

I just turned five. My eyes have trouble moving across a line, so I'm not ready to read yet. But I can hold a pencil with three fingers! I love to sing and pretend and play!

I'm six. I just lost another tooth. Sometimes I get mad at other kids, like when I lose a game. But I'm starting to read. I have a lot of fun with my friends. We play games and tell jokes.

We are our choices.

—Jean-Paul Sartre

SO WHAT DO I TEACH?

An Overview of the Kindergarten Curriculum

What is curriculum? In the broadest sense of the word it means everything about your kindergarten program, including which skills you wish to develop and how you choose to develop them. The way you set up your classroom and how you talk to your students are all curriculum decisions. Good teachers have good reasons for everything they do.

Because schools (and even classrooms within schools) vary in educational beliefs and goals, there is no one "official" kindergarten curriculum. Some schools may have a definite philosophy of education with specific goals and objectives for each teacher to follow. Many schools have general goals and leave it up to the teachers to reach these goals in their own preferred ways. Still other schools have no set curriculum or goals and leave all decisions up to the teacher.

Sometimes we see content curricula mandated by state guidelines (often called frameworks) and also by county or district boards of education. In many cases schools are in a period of transition, as states and school districts create new curricula in keeping with current legislation and/or research. All teachers, whether new or seasoned, need to keep informed of current developments and expectations regarding school curriculum.

Some Common Types of Curricula

Some teachers provide a readiness curriculum, believing the goal of kindergarten is to become prepared for first grade. They may refer to a "scope and sequence" of skills and rely on workbooks, phonics worksheets, and whole group instruction. Most of the activities are teacher-directed with a strong orientation to "task."

A child-centered approach to kindergarten is grounded in child development theory about how children learn. There are more student-directed activities and play is valued as an essential medium for learning.

An integrated approach to curriculum recognizes how growth and development in one domain affect learning in other domains. Some teachers use this understanding to develop a thematic curriculum. In a thematic curriculum, the activities in all content areas are centered around one central theme, or unit.

The literature from the National Association for the Education of Young Children (NAEYC) focuses on the developmentally appropriate curriculum. There is no one right way to provide a developmentally appropriate kindergarten, but there are certain guidelines to follow.

The Developmentally Appropriate Curriculum

A developmentally appropriate curriculum is one which is right for the students' stages of development. The emphasis is on growth instead of mastery, and all aspects of the children's development are nurtured. Skills are rarely taught in isolation, but are learned within the context of meaningful activities. You will find an emphasis on developmentally appropriate curriculum in this book.

A developmentally appropriate curriculum for five-year-olds

- provides daily opportunities for the children to explore their environment

- allows the children to make choices about their activities

- encourages the children to ask questions, solve problems, and express their thoughts and feelings

- provides materials that can be used in a variety of ways

- has teachers who carefully observe children and their work to assess students' interests, strengths, and needs

- has teachers who value individual children's thinking and efforts by displaying their work and incorporating their ideas

- is designed to meet the needs and interests of the children

- is not a "scaled-down" first-grade program

Many kindergarten programs have been evaluated for their developmental appropriateness by the NAEYC. If you are interested in receiving accreditation by the NAEYC, you may call 800-424-2460.

Lesson Planning

Learn what students of this age can reasonably be expected to do, and what it is they need and want to do. This information is acquired through learning about child development as well as by daily observation of, and interactions with, your kindergartners.

Write down what your goals are for the students. You could have a combination of many goals, and even some different goals for different children. The main thing is to figure out what you think is most important for these children to "get" from being in your class. Once you know where you're going, it's a lot easier to get there! After you know your goals, you can come up with your objectives.

You will want to have some kind of program in place when the school year begins, even before you know your students. You might decide to have a theme or specific topic of study. However, this isn't necessary. Your goal may simply be to have everyone get to know each other and learn to use the materials. This can be your program, or curriculum, in itself. The academic curriculum can come later, developing gradually according to the children's needs and interests. Your program should also be shaped by your goals for the students.

Questions to Ask Yourself During the Planning Stage

- What are the "Big Ideas" about this topic? What is the main concept here?

- What kinds of learning experiences might the children have while exploring this topic? Are they meaningful?

- In what ways can I integrate the theme across the curriculum, incorporating the major domains of language and literacy, mathematics, science, the arts, physical development, social studies, and personal and social development?

- Will there be variety in the structure of activities? Will there be teacher-directed, child-directed, whole group, small group, and individual activities?

- Have I made provisions for different learning styles? Am I providing activities in each of the eight intelligences (spatial, logical, interpersonal, intrapersonal, musical, kinesthetic, linguistic, and naturalist)?

- Will there be a variety in the location of activities, including indoors, outdoors, and field trip locations?

- How can I involve my student's families, other classrooms, and the general community?

- Have I made provisions for students with varying abilities and needs?

- Have I taken into consideration issues of bias?

- Is there a way I can incorporate a multicultural perspective?

- What materials do I need? Where can I find them? What needs to be prepared?

- What are my needs for space and time?

- Where can I find out more about this topic?

- How will I introduce this theme? Is my idea fun, fresh, and bound to inspire curiosity?

- Is there a particular time frame for this unit of study? How will it connect to successive themes?

- How will I know if the activities are successful? Do I have criteria for evaluation?

- Am I willing to have my plans change and evolve according to the responses, needs, and interests of my students?

Brainstorming

If you decide to focus on a particular topic or theme, it may help to brainstorm everything you can think of about it. Get a big piece of paper and let the storm begin! (If you have an assistant, include him or her.) For example, a brainstorm for the topic of "night" might look something like the illustration on page 8.

Note that this almost resembles the shape of a spider's web. Some teachers use a curriculum web model.

7

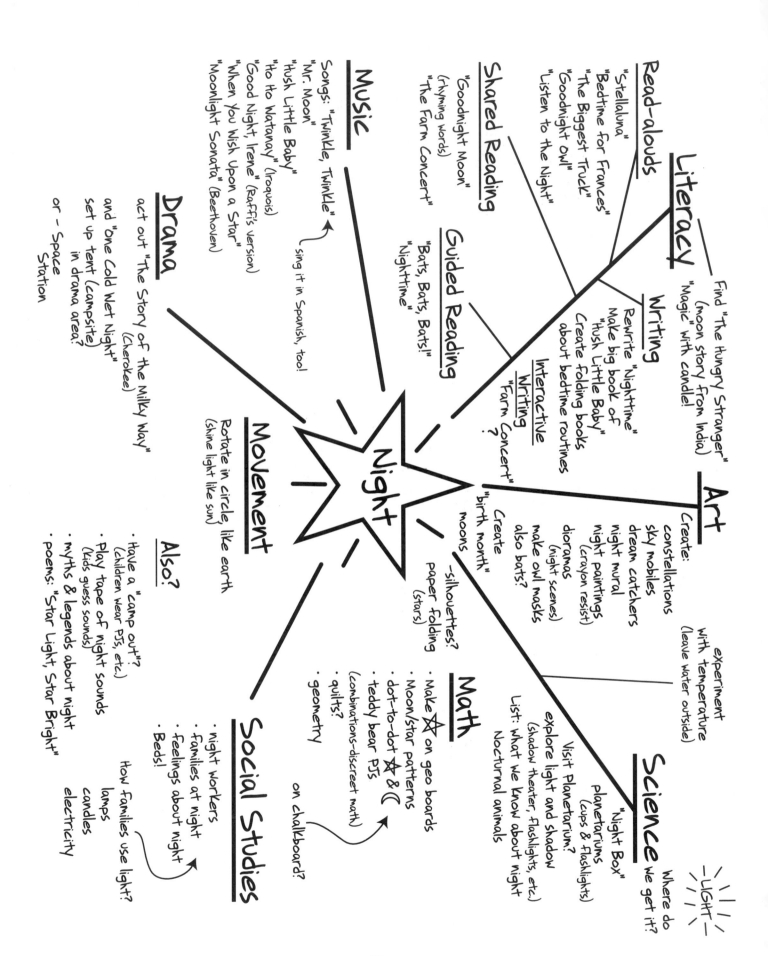

Night

Literacy

Read-alouds
- "Stellaluna"
- "Bedtime for Frances"
- "The Biggest Truck"
- "Goodnight Owl"
- "Listen to the Night"

Find "The Hungry Stranger" (moon story from India) "Magic" with candle!

Shared Reading
- "Goodnight Moon" (rhyming words)
- "The Farm Concert"

Writing
- Rewrite "Nighttime"
- Make big book of "Hush Little Baby"
- Create folding books about bedtime routines

Guided Reading
- "Bats, Bats, Bats!"
- "Nighttime"

Interactive Writing
"Farm Concert"?

Music

Songs: "Twinkle, Twinkle"
"Mr. Moon"
"Hush Little Baby"
"Ho Ho Watanay" (Iroquois)
"Good Night, Irene" (Raffi's version)
"When You Wish Upon a Star"
"Moonlight Sonata" (Beethoven)

→ sing it in Spanish, too!

Drama

act out "The Story of the Milky Way" (Cherokee)

and "One Cold Wet Night"
set up tent (campsite) in drama area?

or – Space Station

Movement

Rotate in circle like earth (shine light like sun)

Also?
- Have a "camp out"? (children wear PJs, etc.)
- Play tape of night sounds (kids guess sounds)
- myths & legends about night
- poems: "Star Light, Star Bright"

Social Studies
- night workers
- families at night
- Feelings about night
- Beds!

How families use light?
→ lamps
candles
electricity

Math
- Make ☆ on geo boards
- Moon/star patterns
- dot-to-dot ☆ & ☾
- teddy bear PJs (combinations-discreet math)
- quilts?
- geometry

on chalkboard?

Art

Create:
- constellations
- sky mobiles
- dream catchers
- night mural
- night paintings (crayon resist)
- dioramas (night scenes)
- make owl masks
- also bats?

Create "birth month" moons

-silhouettes? paper folding (stars)

Science

experiment with temperature (leave water outside)

"Night Box"

Visit Planetarium? Planetariums (cups & flashlights)

List: what we know about night
Nocturnal animals

explore light and shadow (shadow theater, flashlights, etc.)

Where do we get it?

-LIGHT-

CHAPTER TWO: BRINGING THE CURRICULUM TO LIFE

The Big Seven

One way to view the kindergarten curriculum is to divide it into the seven main learning domains. They are: personal and social development, language and literacy, mathematical thinking, scientific thinking, social studies, the arts, and physical development. In kindergarten these domains are interrelated and are continually overlapping. The learning that takes place in one domain often influences growth in the other domains.

Some areas of study, such as health, are placed in different domains by different educators. Some put health with science, others with physical development. Safety is sometimes with social studies, other times with physical development.

Numerous resources are available for teachers. These include professional journals such as *Young Children*, published by the National Association of Educators of Young Children and *Teaching Children Mathematics*, published by the National Council of Teachers of Mathematics (NCTM). You may find excellent resources in teacher supply stores and catalogs, bookstores, and at publisher exhibits at teacher conferences. Other sources include school and town libraries, and teacher preparatory college libraries and stores.

Your most important resource is other teachers. Your colleagues are potential resources for some of the most successful techniques, activities, and insights you will ever receive.

PERSONAL AND SOCIAL DEVELOPMENT

The emotional and social development of your kindergartners may be the most important part of your kindergarten program. Children may be able to count to 100 and say the alphabet, but if they lack confidence or fight with others, their academic lives will be limited and troubled.

The children who enter your classroom have different backgrounds and different temperaments. Some are bursting with self-esteem and enthusiasm, while others may be anxious or even angry. Whatever the case, they all need a loving and sensitive teacher who gives them the important sense of belonging.

- Greet them warmly each day.

- Learn their names by the second day of school if possible.

- Sit at their level and make eye contact.

- Touch them. (Though this is a sensitive topic, you should never be afraid to give a little pat, hug, or handshake. Human touch is vital to life, and some children are starving for it.)

- Take the time to listen to them.

- Remember what's important to them, from family details to favorite hobbies.

- Include their ideas in classroom activities and projects.

- Notice and celebrate their efforts and accomplishments.

- Smile at them.

It is important to remember that self-esteem is a vital part of personal development. Teaching self-esteem is not about indulging children—it is about inspiring them to like and accept themselves. Children with high self-esteem are well-prepared to accept disappointment, face challenges, and deal with frustration. They are likely to share and cooperate with others. Children who feel good about themselves can resist peer pressure and the urge to blame others for their own mistakes. Teaching children to respect themselves is as important as teaching them to respect others.

Besides developing feelings of self-worth and belonging, other areas of personal development include learning responsibility (being safe with materials and cleaning up), flexibility, and staying on task with an activity. If they don't know already, students should also be learning self-help skills related to dressing, hygiene, and toileting, and approaching new learning situations with interest and curiosity.

A kindergarten curriculum is a social curriculum. Kindergarten is the time and place for children to come together, many for the first time, to share space, materials, and ideas. This is when they work on learning to wait, share, take turns, and cooperate with others. Conflicts that arise are viewed as opportunities to learn and practice important social skills.

The time you spend creating a positive social climate in your classroom will be time well spent, especially if you start on the very first day of school and continue throughout the year. Spend the first few weeks (or more) building a "classroom community" of children who are respectful and caring. Your students will be much better prepared for the academic curriculum when they understand expectations for behavior, know how to function in a group, and feel motivated to learn along with their classmates. Remember, social development is an ongoing process. Keep realistic expectations and retain your sense of humor!

> **Taking an interest in what students are thinking and doing is often a much more powerful form of encouragement than praise.**
>
> **—Robert Martin**

Ideas for Promoting Personal and Social Development

Child of the Week

Consider having a Child of the Week or V.I.P. (Very Important Person) program in which each child has a chance to be in the spotlight. During his or her special time, the child has a chance to be the class "Special Helper." He or she may bring in items to share and have family members and pets visit. Some teachers have a V.I.P. schedule and send home a letter to the parents before a child's turn, informing them of the details and inviting them to send in photos to display or a favorite snack to share. A reproducible V.I.P. paper that parents can help complete is on page 90.

Positive Comments

Children should have a turn to hear from their peers how wonderful and special they are. There are many ways to do this, such as having positive statements or thank-you's at the end of the day. You can also draw a large heart or the child's silhouette on a big piece of paper and have everyone take turns saying something special about this classmate. You may need to model this by giving many appropriate examples. Encourage unique, specific, and positive comments with each new person! This could be done during each child's V.I.P. week.

Special Songs

Sing songs daily that include the children's names and their ideas. For example, you can sing the traditional "Bingo," using children's names in place of Bingo's.

Individual Responsibility

Assign responsibilities to your students. Kindergartners love to help, and they learn a variety of skills when they do jobs around the classroom. These include passing out papers, delivering attendance information to the office, watering the plants, feeding the pets, and collecting the jump ropes. As with anything, they need to be shown how to perform these tasks.

Group Rule-making

Discuss rules and consequences with your students. Guide them into developing ideas about how to have a safe and fun classroom. They will understand the rules better and be more invested in them than if you simply posted a list of rules on the first day of school. This simple rule covers many important areas in kindergarten, "Treat others the way you want to be treated."

Class Meetings

Have class meetings where students can express feelings and resolve problems. They can learn to state their concerns, listen to the "other side," and get problem-solving ideas from their classmates. Always end these meetings on a positive note!

> **Children have more need of models than of critics.**
>
> —Joubert

The love of learning,
   the sequestered nooks,
And all the sweet serenity of books.

—Henry Wadsworth Longfellow

LANGUAGE AND LITERACY

The children who walk into your classroom at the beginning of the school year already know a great deal about language, reading, and writing. Even though your students will vary in their knowledge, development, and home environment, they are all experienced users of language. In addition to being active speakers and listeners, your students will have observed people using environmental print such as signs and labels. As their teacher, your job is to recognize and celebrate their vast storehouses of knowledge and to build on this learning with challenging and meaningful literacy experiences.

Although literacy goals may vary from school to school, it is generally accepted that the skills and concepts children learn in kindergarten include:

- listening to conversations and discussions and contributing their ideas clearly

- using language for a variety of purposes

- listening to stories with enjoyment and comprehension

- independently choosing books and other literacy activities

- understanding basic concepts about print, such as directionality

- recognizing the relationship between the spoken and written word

- learning to identify the uppercase and lowercase letters of the alphabet

- developing an understanding of the sounds made by letters (phonemic awareness)

- using drawings and letters (or letter-like shapes) to express ideas or tell stories.

There are many ways to help children develop their literacy skills, and teachers usually refine their own methods as a result of years of experience. Explore the methods and activities presented in this book. Experiment, fine-tune and rearrange. Eventually, you will decide what works best for you and your students. Teaching reading and writing should be a joyful process that allows for exploration and discovery. It should keep the child, and not a list of skills, at the center of the curriculum.

Tips for a Successful Reading Program

Avoid Assumptions
Build on each child's experience. Avoid making assumptions about what each student knows or doesn't know. Some children will never have held a book before, while others may be reading fluently. Prepare to meet the needs of each individual.

Stimulate Interest
Surround students with meaningful and enjoyable print such as song charts, labels, and a variety of books. Resist providing too much at first. As children become familiar with texts and materials, gradually add more material.

Provide a variety of materials and experiences. Set up a writing center with many types of paper, pens, crayons, and pencils.

Make It Meaningful
Involve students in meaningful reading and writing activities. Write a morning message to them, help them write the rules for the block area they created, publish a class poem they wrote, and/or write song words on a chart.

Support students in all their efforts to achieve literacy, regardless of their level of development. If their journal writing is scribbles or their "reading" of a book is really memorization, happily accept it as an important part of the literacy acquisition process.

Be Selective

Evaluate packaged reading programs that come your way, whether expensive basal series or computer programs. Determine how well they match your idea of how children learn to read and write.

Some schools and districts will require you to use a certain reading program or textbook series. Enrich the series with your classroom library of print media.

Regularly perform a "reality check" to see if your program is really meeting the goals you have set for your students. Are the activities meaningful and age-appropriate? Do the children look forward to the activities? Are you having fun, too?

Read, Read, Read!

Read *to* your students, read *for* your students, read *with* your students!

Activities for Language and Literacy Development

The Importance of Language

Before successful reading and writing activities can take place, the classroom must be filled with the sound of language. That is, it should be alive with the happy hum of children talking, singing, chanting, debating, joking, questioning, and exclaiming. Kindergartners will exhibit the wide array of vocal expressions that make us human! Your voice should be heard, too, as you sing, laugh, ask thoughtful questions, share ideas and concerns, and guide the children through the day.

A language-rich environment is one in which all children feel secure enough to speak and express their feelings. Their ideas are safe from ridicule.

In a language-rich environment, students have a say in how something should be done. They are encouraged to resolve their conflicts verbally. Group discussions and sharing are regular practices. Listen to the children with sincere interest.

A language-rich environment is also one that incorporates all types of language and its expressions. Words are used for a variety of purposes, whether to give directions or tickle the funny bone. The atmosphere is filled with stories, songs, poems, chants, and word games, which are not limited to English only. Kindergarten activities naturally lend themselves to language enrichment, as teachers provide meaningful activities that inspire children to express themselves verbally. For example, the act of cutting open a pumpkin can elicit a great deal of language as children describe the "cool orange skin," "slippery seeds," or "musty, sweet smell."

Documenting Language

One of the earliest literacy activities you can provide is a written account of students' language. As the children talk about a recent field trip or decide to send a get-well letter, write down their words on a large piece of paper. Or perhaps students could generate a group poem using the words and phrases expressed during the pumpkin activity mentioned earlier. While taking dictation, resist the urge to correct grammar or story facts. When we write down the child's genuine words, we have an accurate record of his or her "true" language. This is just one of the many ways for children to learn that their words are valued, that writing has purposes, and that there is a connection between spoken and written words.

Book-on-a-Hook

This activity, adapted from Australian educator Sylvia Ashton-Warner, is an excellent choice for kindergarten because it is individualized and honors the interests of the child. It also promotes the development of language, letter recognition, handwriting skills, phonemic awareness, and various conventions of print while using the auditory, visual, tactile, and kinesthetic modalities. It teaches and assesses children and can be used at all stages of literacy development.

Here's what you need:

- plain paper folded in half and stapled along the fold, with a hole punched in the top left-hand corner to form a book (Two pieces will give you a six-page book, enough for three word entries.)

- word cards, about 3 x 6 inches, made from oak tag, or index cards, with a hole punched in the upper left corner of each one (You'll need about six cards per child to start.)

- metal rings to bind the cards (one per child)

- hooks of some kind to hang the books and word cards on

- pencils, crayons, ballpoint pen, and one felt-tip marker (If you don't have all the materials, it's okay to adapt and improvise!)

Here's how it works:

1. Working with one to three children at a time, ask a student to think of a special word that he or she likes or is thinking about. Some children may need ideas to get started.

2. When you say the word back to the child, emphasize the beginning sound. Ask if he or she can tell you the first letter.

3. Use a pencil to write the child's word at the bottom of the first page of his or her book. As you write the word, see if the child can predict what the letters will be. Affirm his or her efforts—"Yes, it does have a *k* sound, but *cake* begins with a *c*."

4. Be sure the child is sitting right next to you watching you form the letters. As you make each letter, either identify it or ask the child to identify it for you. It's a good way to find out what letters the child knows!

5. After you have written the word, ask the child to trace over the word with his or her finger, naming each letter. Then give a pen to the child so that he or she may trace over your writing. While this is happening, you can be helping another child.

6. After the student has traced the word, he or she uses crayons to draw a picture of the word above the word.

7. The child then dictates a story about the word. He or she watches you write the story in pencil on the page opposite the drawing.

8. Read the story back to the child, pointing to each word.

9. Ask the child to spell the word to you so you can write it on the word card. This reinforces letter and word recognition and lets you know how well the child retained what was just learned!

10. As you repeat the activity, with new words, be sure to have the student review what he or she has already learned. Keep the word ring and book on a hook in a convenient location. They should be available for other writing activities as well.

> ## TIP!
>
> *Use the same color marker every time you write on a word card. This helps a child to focus on the letters and structure of the word to figure it out, instead of having his or her memory jogged by the color of the word!*

The best activities for language and literacy development are those that teach and reinforce skills while the children are engaged in meaningful activities. Isolated "focus" lessons can be useful, but they shouldn't comprise the bulk of your kindergarten curriculum.

The Morning Message
One very effective literacy activity is the morning message. This daily activity can teach a variety of skills. On chart paper or the chalkboard, write a message of welcome to the children. The message can state what day it is and what the main activities of the day will be. Special events like birthdays can be added. Some teachers add a daily question or "puzzler." If you use simple, predictable language each day, the children will learn to read the message with great pride. When the children are ready, you can leave off letters or whole words and have students complete the words, identify the missing letters, and finish the message!

If you teach an afternoon class, just change the name to something like "daily message," or "afternoon message."

The Importance of Reading

Read Aloud
Research shows that the single most important factor in learning to read is being read to. Read to your students every day, choosing a variety of books (fiction, nonfiction, and poetry). Include books that connect to the children's real world as well as those that fire their imaginations. Remember that books can be a mirror in which your students see themselves, as well as a window into the minds and lives of others. Folk tales from various cultures, humorous books, fairy tales, serious stories dealing with important issues (such as sibling jealousy or the death of a pet), nature books, and even chapter books are all important to include.

Since you are a teacher, you probably love books yourself. Your enjoyment should show through your voice, facial expressions, and body language. Practice reading the book aloud prior to reading to the children. Don't be afraid to ham it up. The more dramatic you are (changing your voice, pausing, putting your face up close to one of your students) the more engaged your audience will be. Showing your students how to love books and words is one of the greatest gifts you can give them.

Reading Activities

Shared Reading
The shared-reading experience uses enlarged print media, which enables the whole group to follow along as you read. While in read-alouds you might focus more on prediction, language, plot, or character, in shared reading you attend more closely to the print. Enlarged print books (known as big books) and charts of poems or songs are very useful for this activity. Use text that is simple and predictable. During shared reading you can demonstrate voice-print match, directionality and return sweep using a pointer to move from the end of a line of print down and left to the next line. You can also emphasize punctuation, while heightening the children's phonemic awareness and ability to recognize high-frequency words.

Free Reading
Free reading is when children choose their books and read by themselves or with a friend. In kindergarten this can mean talking about the pictures, reading from memory, inventing text, or actually reading the words!

Paired Reading
Paired reading, sometimes known as reading buddies, can mean reading with older students from another class. "Big kids" love reading to kindergartners, and some of your students will be eager to read to the "big kids!"

Read-Along
Read-Along is when the children look at their own copies of a book while listening to the words being read. Often this is done at the listening center. Story tapes are available with audio signals that tell the children when to turn the pages.

Guided Reading
Guided Reading is an activity in which a small group of children (who are reading at the same developmental level and have multiple copies of the same text) learn various reading strategies from their teacher. This can be an effective method for children who are ready to read, but finding the time in a half-day kindergarten without sacrificing other learning experiences may prove challenging.

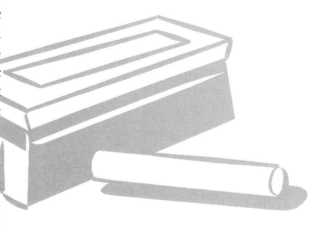

> **Learn as much by writing as by reading.**
>
> —Lord Acton

The Importance of Writing

Writing is one of our most important ways of communicating. In order to learn how to write, children need daily, meaningful opportunities to write. Just as children learn to read by reading, children learn to write by writing.

Writing should be purposeful. This means that the various kinds of writing that children do in kindergarten should be done for "real-life" reasons, such as expressing feelings, communicating ideas, or creating important lists of things to remember. These kinds of writing activities will have much more meaning to students than filling out worksheets. When we expand our definition of writing to include all the marks and "scribbles" we find in kindergarten, then writing can certainly begin in the first few days of school. Don't wait until after you have "taught" the alphabet or given handwriting lessons.

Writing can take place anywhere and anytime in the classroom. Not only can your students write in the writing center you've provided for them, but they can write in the science center, block area, and dramatic play area as well. If you provide materials such as paper, clipboards, markers, journals, and clothespins (for hanging up signs and labels), they will put them to good use! You will delight in seeing students create signs for their block constructions, shopping lists in the housekeeping area, and predictions in the science center. Children will become quite comfortable "inventing" their own spelling or copying words from various sources around the room.

Writing Activities

Interactive Writing

Interactive writing involves students and their teacher creating text together. There is a purpose to the writing as students compose letters to pen pals, recipes, story rewrites, or descriptions of recent experiences. Together the teacher and the children negotiate the text. There is discussion about how to spell many of the words, and both the teacher and the children print the words using conventional spelling. It can take several sessions to finish the text.

Shared Writing

Shared writing involves the teacher doing all the printing while the group suggests ideas about text and spelling. This activity can be as short as writing a word or two on the message board, or be as involved as composing a thank-you letter to a recent visitor or listing "what we wonder" about spiders. Both shared writing and interactive writing provide excellent opportunities to teach phonemic awareness, letter formation, conventional spelling, and concepts about print. They also provide you with information about the children as readers, writers, and speakers.

Journal Writing

Journal writing varies from class to class, but usually entails the children writing a page or two in a book of some kind. Journal entries tend to be personal accounts of the students' experiences, but this can vary. Some teachers have their students write daily in their journals (maybe during the

I LOVE MY DOG BEKES HE EZ NIS TO ME. MY DOG BARKZ AT PEPL

first ten minutes after they walk in the door), while others make it a weekly activity or choice. Some kindergarten journals have plain paper, others lined. An example of a journal page is illustrated below. Most teachers encourage invented spelling for journal writing, as this "frees" the children to write without worrying about spelling correctly.

A quick conference with the children after they write can provide an opportunity to discuss and support their work ("You used a lot of red and orange for the fire. That makes it so hot!"). You can use this as an opportunity to nudge a student to the next step ("Your picture is of a boat. If you were going to write 'boat,' how would you start? Want to give it a try?"). Some teachers choose to write the "real" text (what the child intends the words to say) underneath the picture or writing. Other types of journal writing include math journals and science (or "discovery") journals, in which children write and/or draw their ideas, observations, solutions and discoveries.

Writing Workshop

Writing Workshop tends to be a structured time for the group to write stories in the form of books. The teacher presents a mini-lesson on an aspect of writing (how to write "by" on the cover, how to approach invented spelling, the importance of detail in the illustrations, etc.). Then the children write their stories. Some children will quickly scribble their way through their books; others will spend days on one illustration. Conferencing is done with the children as they work on their stories. As with journal writing, children are encouraged to write the sounds they hear when they say the word aloud. Students will need help and encouragement while learning how to carry out this complex task.

Some teachers prefer to keep the stories in writing folders all year long so the children (as well as the teachers and parents) can see the development of their writing. Often a comment sheet is stapled in the folder to keep track of the student's progress. This serves as a great tool for assessing each child's

growth. Other items to have in the writing workshop folder are a manuscript chart (page 48), My Alphabet and Number Page (page 21), and a list of topic ideas which children and parents can write about together at home.

Many teachers work with their students on editing a favorite story so that it can be published (typed and bound). Publishing their own books can be a real thrill for students (and their parents). Some classes even have publishing parties! In addition to making individual books, children can each create one page for a big class book. For example, after reading Joy Cowley's *Mrs. Wishy-Washy* (The Wright Group, 1990), a story about three farm animals who love mud, children can think of other animals that jump in the mud, ("Oh lovely mud," said the stegosaurus.) The entire class will love to read the book together many times.

Providing small books with familiar text for students to illustrate is another fun literacy activity. These include simple stories, songs, and poems. For example, try reproducing the *Rain* book on pages 22 and 23. After the children have learned the poem from an enlarged print copy on a chart, they can make their own books. They can illustrate each page and create their own rainy covers by painting with watercolors on an extra sheet of paper which can be stapled to the front of the book.

In a literature response activity, students create something after hearing a story. This can include dramatizing the story, painting a mural inspired by the story, or rewriting the story. Rewrites are effective because students are writing within a familiar structure. For example, after becoming familiar with Bill Martin's *Brown Bear, Brown Bear, What Do You See?* (H. Holt & Co., 1992), children can create smaller versions of the book, inventing different animals that see each other. You could even have the books pre-made with space for drawings and blank lines where the animal names should be written.

More Literacy Tips

Use a pocket chart for reading activities, such as matching up the rhyming words from books or poems such as Margaret Wise Brown's *Goodnight Moon* (HarperCollins, 1997).

Make games from a variety of materials. You can cut up sentence strips and have the students reassemble them. Index cards are useful for letter or word matching games. Students can find, match, and name letters or words using magnetic letters. They can also guess which magnetic letter they are touching by feeling it with their eyes closed. Little toys or pictures can be matched by beginning letter or categorized into rhyming pairs.

Develop language skills by playing "I Spy" and other games that require children to use descriptive language. A child can create a simple pattern block design and hide it from view while explaining to other students how to make it.

Strengthen listening skills by playing games such as "Telephone" and "Simon Says."

Provide a variety of materials that exposes your students to the alphabet, such as charts, ABC books, letter stencils, alphabet stamps, and puzzles.

TIP!

Avoid getting involved in the popular "whole language vs. phonics" debate. Teachers who correctly apply whole-language theory do incorporate phonics!

Have a "reading tub" containing word puzzles, magnetic letters, and ABC games that children can use if they're waiting for their turn with you for "teacher time."

Label items in the classroom. Children can help!

Use a listening center. Children can share books if you can't get enough copies. Reading along with a tape helps children learn to read, and it frees you to be with others.

Use a magnetic board and letters to help students learn letter names, as well as for matching upper and lower letters, grouping similar letters, and constructing high-frequency words that appear in their shared or guided reading lessons.

Consider providing your students with opportunities to write at home. Children can have turns taking home writing boxes with paper, markers, and other supplies. They can also share the use of a stuffed toy accompanied by a journal. Students can draw, write, or dictate what this visiting friend does when in their homes.

Always keep in mind that not all activities are appropriate for all students. Because you may have children able to read sentences with ease and others who aren't even sure how to spell their names, your curriculum must be able to accommodate everyone's needs. The beauty of these activities and materials is that they can be adapted to meet the needs of every student.

> **The limits of my language mean the limits of my world.**
>
> —Ludwig Wittgenstein, <u>Tractatus Logico-Philosophies</u>

Name _____

My ABC Poem

A B   C D E

School   is   where   we   like   to   be.

F   G   H I J

School   is   where   we   work   and   play.

K L   M N O

Every   day   we   learn   and   grow.

P Q   R S T

School   is   fun   for   you   and   me.

U V   W X Y

There   is   nothing   we   won't   try.

Z Z   Z   Z   Z

School   is   where   we   like   to   be!

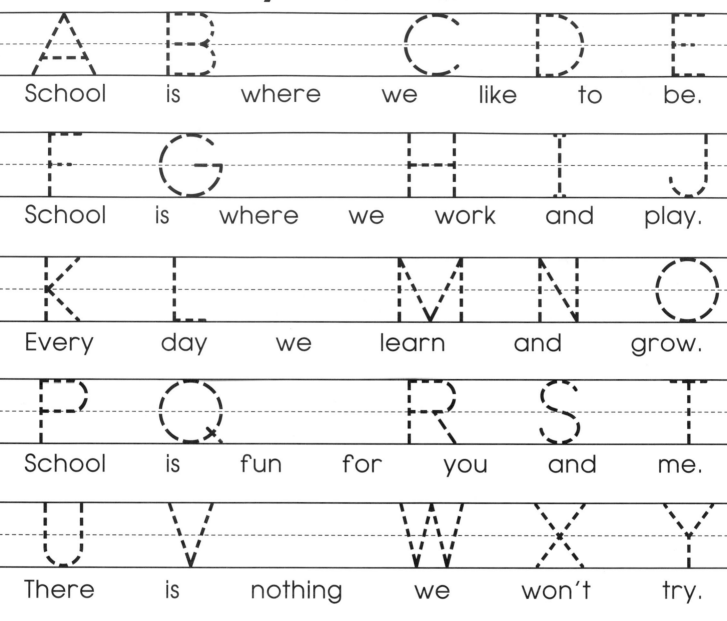

Name _____

My Alphabet and Number Page

Aa apple	Bb butterfly	Cc cat	Dd dog	Ee egg	Ff fish
Gg glasses	Hh house	Ii igloo	Jj jack-o-lantern	Kk kite	Ll leaf
Mm mittens	Nn nest	Oo octopus	Pp pig	Qq queen	Rr rainbow
Ss sun	Tt turtle	Uu umbrella	Vv valentine	Ww whale	Xx x-ray
Yy yo-yo	Zz zebra	1 one	2 two	3 three	4 four
5 five	6 six	7 seven	8 eight	9 nine	10 ten

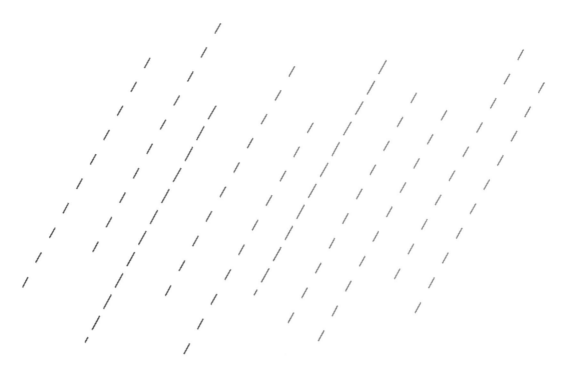

Rain on my house.

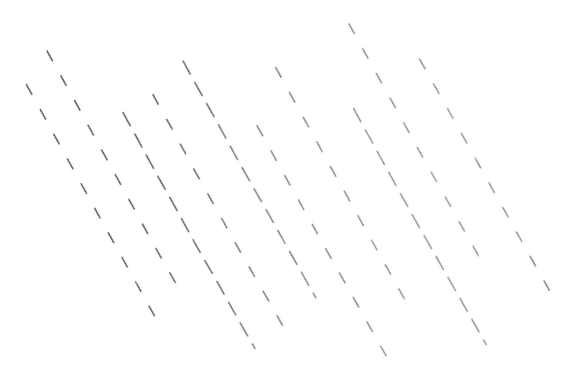

Rain on my umbrella.

FS122002 Getting Ready to Teach Kindergarten

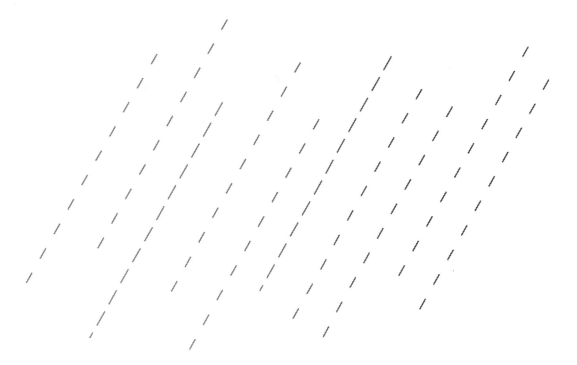

Rain on my tree.

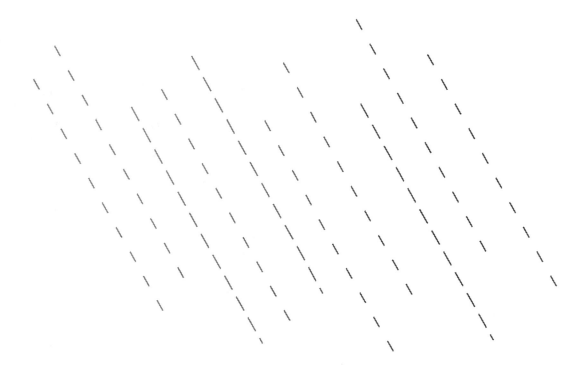

But not on me!

MATHEMATICAL THINKING IN KINDERGARTEN

Goals

Some exciting changes are occurring in the way kindergarten children are learning mathematics. The focus is on providing students with opportunities to try different approaches to "real life" problems. Kindergartners are encouraged to communicate with others about their reasoning. In the most innovative classrooms, students actively engage in counting, classifying, investigating, comparing, and solving a variety of problems using manipulatives such as blocks, buttons, color tiles, shells, and teddy bear counters. These rooms are filled with "math talk" as students share their discoveries, compare their ideas, and work together to come up with solutions.

Mathematical goals will vary from school to school, but it is reasonable to expect most of your students to learn to:

- solve mathematical problems using different strategies

- use words to explain mathematical ideas

- recognize, duplicate, and extend patterns

- count objects, using one-to-one correspondence

- understand relationships between quantities (more, less, equal)

- sort objects into subgroups

- collect and record data

- make reasonable estimates of quantity, volume, length, etc.

- begin to identify the numerals 0–20

- begin to write the numerals 0–10

Developing Mathematical Thinking

Mathematical concepts and skills are reinforced throughout the kindergarten day as children explore, play, and carry out their daily classroom routines. Children develop their spatial sense as they build with blocks, practice their estimation skills when cutting yarn for a project, and learn one-to-one correspondence when figuring out how many cups to put out for snack time.

They learn about measurement when they cook, subtraction when they sing "Five Little Monkeys," and problem-solving when faced with fewer cookies than students. An alert teacher looks for opportunities for learning ("teachable moments") and pays attention to how his or her students are using mathematics in the classroom.

"I wonder why...?"

"What would happen if...?"

"Tell me about your pattern."

"Can you do it another way?"

These inviting words give students the freedom to be creative, the confidence to solve problems, and the power to do mathematics. When you give your students the opportunity to construct their own knowledge, you are opening the doors of mathematics to all young learners.

This is the challenge. This is the vision.

—Miriam A. Leiva, Curriculum and Evaluation Standards for School Mathematics, Addenda Series

Tips for Bringing Math To Life

Offer Variety

Provide your students with lots of math materials. A math center with counting games, number puzzles, manipulatives, balance scales, and counting books is always popular. Keep on hand various objects for patterning, sorting, counting, and measuring. Integrate materials in other parts of the classroom, such as measuring cups in the water table, coins in the drama center, and paper shapes in the art center.

Vary the types of math experiences you offer students. Give them opportunities to approach math tasks in different ways. Usually the same skill or concept can be taught in a variety of ways. For example, counting can be practiced on the playground when skipping rope, singing "This Old Man," doing the calendar, or stringing beads. Some math lessons will be teacher-directed, others student-directed. There will be cooperative group work and individual math tasks. Children learn in different ways. When you vary how you teach, you increase their chances for success.

Make Math Real

Help your students see the relevance of math to their daily lives. The most effective math activities are those which are "real" and meaningful to children. Plan lessons accordingly and take advantage of what is occurring naturally in the classroom. For example, let the children figure out how many milks to get for snack, or estimate how many cookies will be needed for Open House.

Challenge Students

Provide learning experiences that are challenging yet achievable. Children like to be challenged to think and explore new ideas, especially if they're interested and confident. You don't want bored, uninspired students, so be prepared to stretch their thinking by posing questions ("Can you tell me why you did it that way?" or "Can you think of another way to do it?").

Provide Music

Play classical music during math activities. Recent research on the brain and learning has shown that performance on mathematical tasks (especially those related to spatial awareness) improve when listening to certain classical music, especially that of Mozart and Bach.

Be Patient

Be aware of children who are struggling. An alert teacher notices the children who appear confused or uncomfortable with a task, and takes the time to find the cause. If a child isn't grasping a concept or developing a skill, he or she may need to learn in a different way. Some children just need more time to use materials before concepts can be integrated. In rare cases, a child may have a learning problem that requires special assistance.

Check It Out!

Explorations for Early Childhood by Lalie Harcourt (Addison-Wesley, 1988)

Investigations in Number, Data and Space: Mathematical Thinking in Kindergarten by Karen Economopoulos and Megan Murray (Dale Seymour Publications, 1998). This book is part of a six-book series.

Mathematics Their Way: An Activity-Centered Mathematics Program for Early Childhood Education by Mary Baratta-Lorton (Addison-Wesley, 1976)

Teaching Children Mathematics, a journal published by the National Council of Teachers of Mathematics, 1906 Association Drive, Reston, VA 20191-1593

We must go beyond what we were taught and teach how we wish we had been taught. We must bring to life a vision of what a mathematics classroom should be . . . A richer mathematics program is also supported by an explosion of new mathematical knowledge—more mathematics has been created in this century than in all our previous history.

—Miriam A. Leiva, Curriculum and Evaluation Standards for School Mathematics, Addenda Series

Math Activities

Free Exploration

Young children must have frequent opportunities to enjoy math materials in their own ways before performing a specific task with them. You can discover a lot about how your students learn by observing how they explore and manipulate materials. Putting out tubs of pattern blocks, cubes, bottle caps, shells, buttons, or keys will provide the children with hours of discovery in a relaxed, playful atmosphere.

Sorting

The ability to group objects is an important conceptual skill that builds a foundation for patterning and graphing. Discussing the attributes of objects enriches vocabulary and strengthens visual awareness. Students can sort just about anything in the room, including themselves! Kindergartners love "people sorting." Choose a student to sort the people in the class by a secret rule such as hair color, types of clothes, or glasses/no glasses. Have other students guess the "secret rule." Model more complex ways to sort materials (by texture, by source, or use of items) and have students guess your rule to expand student awareness and inspire them to go beyond the usual size and color groupings.

Patterning

Recognizing and creating patterns are requisite skills in mathematics. Children need regular opportunities to explore the concept of repetition of a sequence. Take your kindergartners on a "pattern walk" around the school and they will enjoy finding repeating features in brick walls, windows, and fences. They can make "people patterns" with their own bodies (standing, standing, sitting), and sound patterns with musical instruments or their hands (clap, pat, clap, pat). Linking cubes are useful for creating color patterns. Pasta, buttons, rubber stamps, toothpicks, and many other materials can be used for pattern-making. Children not only love to create patterns, but enjoy pointing out that patterns are everywhere!

Counting and Number Activities

Your kindergarten day is filled with opportunities to count, such as taking attendance and counting the days on the calendar. Your class can also play a variety of games that involve counting and number recognition, and sing songs that have counting and various number operations. Children need daily opportunities to count real objects in order to develop their one-to-one correspondence skills and to develop a sense of quantity (What does a group of six look like? How does it compare to a group of nine?). A good math program consists of infusing math into the daily activities (How many steps is it to the bathroom? If we take giant steps, will the number change? or How many blocks do you think you need for the wall?). A good program also includes planning and implementing specific activities, such as the "Sleeping Bears" activity featured on the next page.

Sleeping Bears
(small group activity)

Materials needed: Six (or whatever number you're working on) teddy bear counters and one plastic bowl (or other opaque container) per child, plus a set of bears and a bowl for the teacher.

Procedure: Have children turn their bowls upside down to make "houses". Have each child put some bears on the roof of the house and hide the rest inside the house. The children take turns telling the group how many bears are on each others' roofs and how many are sleeping inside. The bowls are lifted up to check on how many bears are inside sleeping. Repeat the game several times, making sure students vary the numbers of bears sleeping. As each bear house is slowly raised, have everyone say the number combination together. This is an excellent game for practicing counting skills, and developing the concept of number combinations (3+3=6, 5+1=6, etc.). This game builds a foundation for understanding the relationship between addition and subtraction. (If there are six all together, and only two are on the roof, then how many are left sleeping in the house?) This activity is also an excellent assessment tool!

Spatial Activities

Many activities help children develop their spatial awareness. Large motor activities such as ball games, dance, and movement help children gain a greater sense of how their bodies move through space. Those who have a good sense of balance and sense of equilibrium tend to be able to grasp the concept of symmetry and equality. Daily opportunities to explore shapes on both the two-dimensional level and three-dimensional level are very important. Kindergartners can make shapes with their bodies by themselves and cooperatively with others. They also need to build with unit blocks, complete shape puzzles, create designs with pattern blocks, and match blocks of different shapes to their 2-D representations on paper. They need practice with estimating and measuring, and with comparing size, length, and volume.

Cooking, sand, and water play are all good for this kind of practice. Experiences that help children see the parts of a whole (such as using pattern blocks to see that three blue rhombuses equal 1 yellow hexagon) will help future understanding of fractions.

Graphing

Graphs are a lot of fun, and some teachers do them every day! Be sure to start with real objects and just two attributes, such as red apples and green apples or shoes with laces and shoes without laces. Children have fun creating their own graphs by collecting data themselves. Students can gather and record information then decide how to group the data as well as whether to represent it in a picture or a bar graph, or in some other way. Discuss each graph—What does the data tell us? Which flavor of ice cream is the most popular? How do you know this? How many more friends have curly hair than straight hair? How can we find out? Include open-ended questions in your discussion by asking what the data tells us. Revisit the graphs throughout the year!

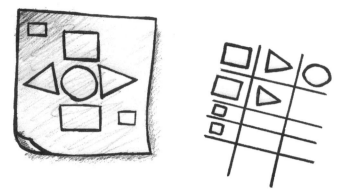

> **A mathematician, like a painter or poet, is a maker of patterns.**
>
> —G.H. Hardy

Graph It!

The reproducible grid on the next page (or your own version of a similar grid) can have many uses in your classroom. The following are just a few ideas to get you started!

Sorting

After several introductory activities where your students begin to investigate how certain things are "alike" or "different," they can start to examine small objects and think of ways to group them by various attributes, including size, shape, color, and texture.

Have children pair up for this activity. Working with a partner will give students opportunities to discuss their observations and explain their reasoning. Provide small containers or bags of little items: buttons, shells, toys, pasta, plastic counters, blocks, seeds, beads, and bottle caps.

Give each child a copy of the worksheet. Explain that each of the rows on the graph represents a group of objects that share similar characteristics. Demonstrate, for example, that one row represents round buttons. The other row represents buttons that are not round.

Have children experiment with their items. Students can begin the project by placing their objects directly on the grid. Later, they may progress to recording the data on the graph by coloring or drawing in the squares.

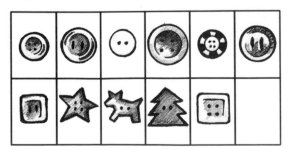

Graphing Data

After students have experimented with the concept of gathering and sorting data, they may want to record and sort their information. Make graphs available so that children can record data that has already been gathered or simply make a record of their own information, such as types of figures in a block construction or pattern.

Gathering Data

Put the graphs on clipboards and have students conduct surveys! First, demonstrate how to mark an "X" or check-mark in a graph box to represent one person. Next, have students ask their classmates specific questions, marking their answers on the graph sheet. For example, students can chart how many classmates are five years old and how many are six years old. They can record how many prefer pumpkin pie and how many prefer apple pie. They can chart the number of boys and the number of girls in the classroom. The possibilities are endless!

X	X	X	X	X	X	X					Blue Eyes
X	X	X	X	X	X	X	X	X				Brown Eyes
X	X	X									Green Eyes

Note that the graph can be modified to meet your needs. You can use it vertically to make columns or horizontally to make rows. To add extra columns, just photocopy the page several times, cut out the number of columns needed and tape them to a copy to make a new master. You can also tape two grids end-to-end to accommodate additional information. You and the students can add your own labels, questions, and lines, as needed.

My Math Graph

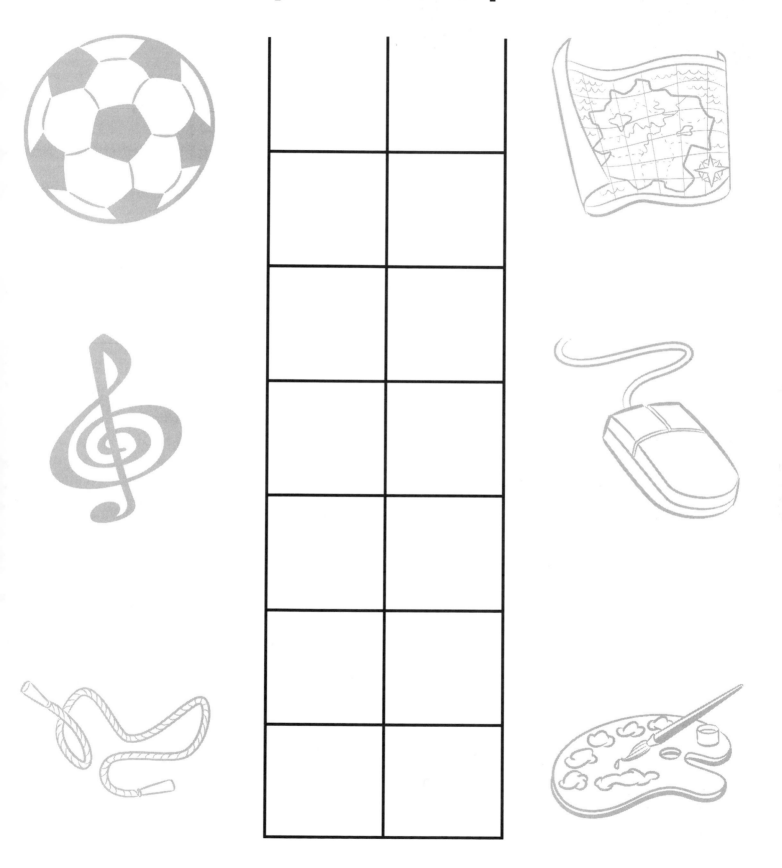

SCIENTIFIC THINKING

Children are natural scientists. They are interested in the world around them, are curious about how things work, and love to explore and manipulate materials to find out more about them. Kindergartners are in the cognitive stage of preoperational thinking and thus need frequent opportunities to handle real (concrete) objects to construct their thinking and perceptions.

You may already have a science curriculum in place at your school, complete with goals, objectives, and kits of materials. You may also have some freedom in deciding which scientific experiences and concepts are important for your children to have. In any case, try to keep it developmentally appropriate and meaningful. (Some curriculum choices may be obvious, such as studying snow in the winter!) Also, try to coordinate with other teachers in your school to avoid repeating the same activities or leaving out key skills.

Another good rule-of-thumb in kindergarten science is to keep it process-oriented. Learning content is important, but the method by which children understand and integrate concepts deserves just as much of our respect and attention. The processes of scientific investigation include:

Observing

By touching, listening, changing, shaking, pouring, and so on, children notice the properties of objects. Teachers can help them articulate their observations, which will include noticing changes, differences, and similarities.

Questioning

Why? How come? What will happen if? These are just a few of the many questions your five-year-old scientists will ask!

> **TIP!**
>
> *WAIT! Studies have shown that when teachers give their students more time to respond to questions (at least 3 to 5 seconds), there is more active participation by students.*

Predicting

Children can learn to make "smart guesses" about the outcome of investigations, especially if you help them be comfortable with risk-taking.

Investigating

With their five senses as well as tools, such as pulleys, magnifying glasses, balance scales, or flashlights, children can find answers to their questions (and, hopefully, come up with more questions!).

Concluding

Children can begin to think of reasons for why certain things happened in their observations and investigations.

Many topics invite young children to explore and learn about the natural and physical worlds. Some favorites include the five senses, weather, plants, animals, insects, marine life, birds, rocks, bones, magnets, light and color, shadows, water, seeds, bubbles, sand and soil, wheels, and pulleys. Changes in our world such as seasons, growth, and life cycles are also worth exploring.

Science Journals

Using discovery journals, students can record their reactions to various scientific objects. You can easily create a science observation reproducible on a blank sheet of paper. To make a picture box, simply draw a large box across the top half of the paper. Beneath the picture box, write the words "This is a picture of" and "I noticed that." Leave space for the student to complete the sentences.

This sheet can be used throughout the year as you explore different themes with your students. Children can draw pictures of the class pet or of flowers they find on a class nature walk. They can use the sheet to chart the growth of a plant. Blank copies can be bound together to make individual journals, or each child's completed observations on a certain subject can be put together to form a class book.

How to Keep Science Alive in Your Classroom

A science center or "discovery table" is a must! A variety of items for the children to explore will inspire curiosity and wonder. Sure hits are colorful rocks, seashells, feathers, kaleidoscopes, nests, and gadgets. Change the items as needed and encourage the children to add their own treasures.

Always have science books and magazines available. They heighten interest, provide information, and are one more way to show the children how much you value science. Be sure to include resources such as the Golden or Audubon nature guides.

Have a "mystery" box, tray, or item that invites the children to guess what something is. The item can be anything from a deer bone or milkweed pod to an antique tool or piece of lava. Hidden items in a box can be felt, shaken, or smelled while the children are trying to make their guesses.

Value your students' scientific questions and discoveries by writing down their words. You can have charts of their ideas, labeled "What We Know About" or "What We Wonder About," as well as displays of their writings and drawings. Science or discovery journals are another good way for children to have their observations recorded.

Surround your students with growing things. Keep plants and nurture a class pet. Rats, fish, and Madagascan hissing roaches are all popular! (You can order the roaches from the Carolina Biological Supply Company at 1-800-334-5551.)

Have the tools for investigation always available. These can include balance scales, magnifying glasses, microscopes, magnets, flashlights, prisms, and funnels. Tubes, pumps, water wheels, eyedroppers, straws, corks, hardware, gears, periscopes, and mirrors will also provide hours of fascination.

Be aware of your environment and of opportunities for discovery. Don't be afraid to drop your "plans" while you run outside to admire a rainbow! Explore the outdoors often. Convey to the children your own sense of wonder. If you are fascinated by worms and curious about magnets, they will be too!

Sure-hit Science Activities

Sure-hit activities include color mixing (colored water and eyedroppers), and snow or crushed ice in the sand table. Walks outdoors can include nature hunts where students collect specimens on masking tape bracelets or listening walks where they observe sounds. Give students color cards (linoleum samples work well) which they can match with colors they find outdoors. Play "What Doesn't Belong?" by scattering non-natural items around before the walk. (Be sure to remove all evidence afterwards!)

Inside the classroom, engage in magnet painting (moving a paint-soaked paper clip by dragging a magnet beneath a sheet of paper). Shadow play with flashlights, colored cellophane, and/or the overhead projector. Use microscopes to investigate poppy seeds, lettuce, sand, and any other item that will fit beneath the lens. Make paper airplanes. Play blindfold "feelie" games (having students identify objects by touch alone). Watch slugs or snails crawl across a clear surface. Experiment with water, mud, bark, and gadgets of all sorts. Make music using instruments you construct in the classroom. Above all, encourage curiosity, adventure, and discovery!

Use the "My Bean Book" reproducible on pages 32 and 33 to get your students excited about science by planting beans and watching them grow!

> **Our young people must be exposed to science both because it is useful and because it is fun. Both of these qualities should be taken at a truly high value.**
>
> **—Edward Teller, Conversations on the Dark Secrets of Physics, 1991**

My Bean Book
by

_____

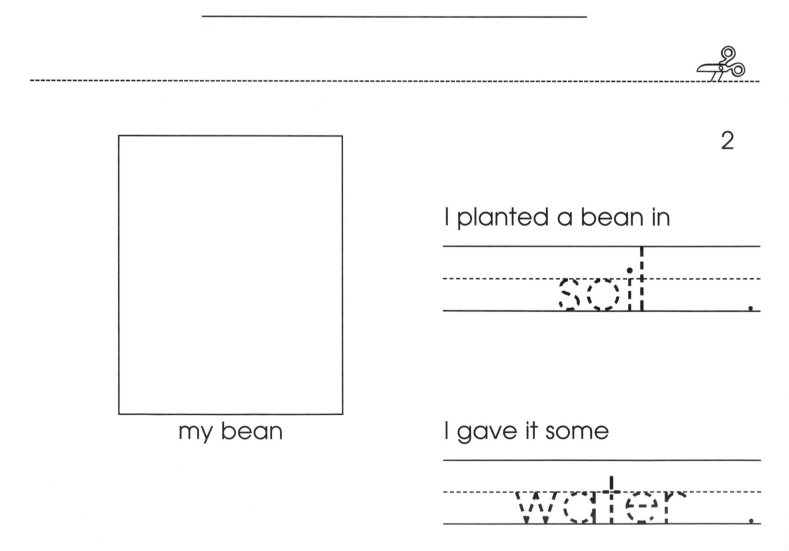

my bean

I planted a bean in

soil .

I gave it some

water .

After _____ days, my bean sprouted.

Now it looks like this.

✂--

After _____ days, I measured my bean plant.

It is _____ inches tall.

SOCIAL STUDIES

Social studies is all about people. It is understanding how people are the same and how they are different, how they live and work, what kinds of things affect people (such as technology and geography), and how people affect the environment. It is learning about rules, rights, and responsibilities. Social studies also includes learning about people in various cultures, both past and present.

The Dramatic Play Area

The dramatic play area or "pretend" corner of your classroom is an excellent area for the children to explore some of these topics in greater depth by role-playing with a variety of materials. For example, children can act out a variety of family roles in the "play house" area, which can include a sink, stove, dishes, dolls, telephones, dress-up clothes, etc. The area can become a grocery store, hospital, animal clinic, post office, teepee, restaurant, and so on. Let the children work together to decide what this area will change into, and get them involved in thinking about how to set it up.

Field Trips

Kindergartners love going on field trips, whether it is a walk to the neighborhood bakery or fire station or a bus ride to a farm in the country. Children learn much more from real places with real people, sights, sounds, and smells than they do from videos or pictures. So take a lot of field trips and be sure to "process" them when you return, through discussions, writing, drawing, and dramatizations. (And a class thank-you letter to your host is always important!)

Visitors

You can invite many people into your classroom to speak to your students about their lives or work. Your students' parents, the school custodian, a local police officer, musician, or scientist are only a few examples of the many people who might be willing to come for a visit. Some people may bring items to show, others may want to lead an activity. When planning visits, try to include a variety of people of different ages, genders, and ethnicities. Look for opportunities to dispel stereotypes.

Other Activities

Young children love to learn about how people live and work together, and the best place to start is right in your classroom. When you and your students work together to create a classroom community, everyone learns about responsibility, cooperation, and interdependence. It is vital that all kindergartners feel they are valued members of the group. They need to have a role in decision-making, including helping to create classroom rules. All children need to help clean and maintain the classroom by performing necessary tasks as needed or doing specific jobs that rotate daily or weekly.

Learn About Ourselves

An excellent social studies topic to focus on early in the year is "ourselves." When children learn about themselves and each other, wonderful things happen. Their own self-awareness is heightened, they get to know their classmates better, and family-like bonds begin to form among the students and you, the teacher. Another benefit is that natural connections can be made with the other learning domains (refer to page 9). The following are a few activities to get you started.

- Create "Happy/Sad" books or masks when exploring feelings.

- Have students study their faces in mirrors and make self-portraits.

- Create a class graph showing class eye colors or favorite colors.

- Mix paint to find colors to match students' skin tones.

- Do body tracing and have students paint themselves using the correct skin color.

- Let students measure themselves and others with string or linking cubes and sort each other by age, hair color, and other traits.

- Sing songs that include their interests and personal features.

- Play "getting to know you" games at circle time. For example, ask students to determine the favorite food of the person to his or her right, then share the answer with the group.

- Listen to a story about brothers and sisters and encourage students to share their own experiences. Count how many people have pets.

- Play guessing games in which students have to figure out which child is being thought of, based on clues. For example, "This person has a turtle." or "This person speaks Spanish."

Learn About Our Needs

Another area of focus in social studies can be "our needs," which you and the children can discuss and list. Talk about the difference between wants (friends, toys, pets) and needs (food, clothing, shelter, air, water).

The basic human needs of food, clothing, and shelter offer a multitude of opportunities for learning. Kindergartners easily relate to these topics as integral parts of their daily lives. You can spend weeks exploring each topic. Here are just a few ideas to get you started.

Food

- Learn about nutrition, food groups and where food comes from.

- Visit a farm, grocery store, or bakery.

- Discover and prepare food from around the world.

- Explore food colors, textures, shapes, and smells.

- Sort and graph favorite foods.

- Look inside foods by cutting them open. Compare seeds and look at lettuce veins under a microscope.

- Grow beans or sprouts.

- Make a book of recipes.

- Read stories about food and prepare some of the dishes discussed. For example, bake gingerbread cookies after reading "The Gingerbread Man." Read Ann McGovern's *Stone Soup* (Scholastic, 1986), then make a pot of soup. Ann Morris's *Bread! Bread! Bread!* (Lothrop, Lee & Shepard, 1993) is also useful.

- Collect food for the needy.

Shelter

- Explore why we need shelters and what is needed inside a shelter.

- Find out how homes can differ according to environment and time period.

- Discuss the various ways people decorate their shelters.

- Create shelters using different materials, such as blocks, sticks, clay, cardboard or plastic foam. Construct tents, teepees, wigwams and box houses.

- Ask children to explore their own homes, counting windows and beds, discovering where the water comes from and how the house is heated. Think of ways to graph this data.

- Investigate houses in the neighborhood, noticing features such as color, shape, size, and number of chimneys or windows.

- Visit a house under construction.

- Learn about plumbing, carpentry, and electricity.

- Read Daniel Pinkwater's *The Big Orange Splot* (Scholastic, 1993), and have children design their own dream houses. Read "Hansel and Gretel" and make candy houses from milk cartons, graham crackers, and frosting.

Clothing

- Discuss why we wear certain types of clothing. Talk about how climate and culture affect our clothing choices. Talk about how clothing styles change over time and according to the weather.

- Compare students' clothing by looking at materials and colors. "People sort" by clothing, looking for zippers, buttons, or pockets. Sort and graph the data.

- Discover how clothing is made. Learn about weaving, sewing, and dyeing.

- Read *The Mitten* by Alvin Tresselt (Scholastic, 1989), an old Ukrainian folk tale.

- Study wool, cotton, latex, and leather under a microscope.

- Use water to observe how raincoat material works.

- Visit a dry cleaner, textile factory, or tailor.

- Study types of headwear people use at work or for special ceremonies.

- Read *Hats! Hats! Hats!* by Ann Morris (Scholastic, 1991). Make hats.

> We can best understand learning as growth, an expanding of ourselves into the world around us. We can also see that there is no difference between living and learning, that living _is_ learning, that it is impossible, and misleading, and harmful to think of them as being separate.
>
> —John Holt, <u>What Do I Do Monday?</u>, 1970

VISUAL AND PERFORMING ARTS

ART

When Albert Einstein said, "Imagination is more important than knowledge," he didn't mean that knowledge is not important. After all, his work was based on his tremendous knowledge of mathematics and physics. But he also recognized that without imagination and creativity, our knowledge takes us virtually nowhere.

The processes of wondering, envisioning, feeling, expressing, risk-taking, and creating are what gave us the work of Mozart, Charlie Chaplin, and Georgia O'Keeffe. Imagination inspired the Brooklyn Bridge, our moon landing, and Martin Luther King, Jr.'s "I Have a Dream" speech.

Art should be an integral part of every kindergarten program. Establishing an effective art program means:

- having art materials available to the children every day

- allowing the children to use the art materials in their own ways

- encouraging children to try different materials and techniques

- noticing opportunities for artistic expression throughout the day (finger-paint anger, watercolor the rain, make tissue collages after reading an Eric Carle book)

- giving some assistance, when wanted and needed, to help children reach their goals ("Do you want an idea about how to get those scissors to work?")

- avoiding judgments (this includes most kinds of praise) about art work

- the process is usually more important than the product

- displaying the children's creations around the room

There is some value to having children occasionally work on a project that involves following directions and seeing a model. The word "craft" is often more suitable in these circumstances.

Art, for art's sake, should be an important part of your program. But also keep in mind the ways you can integrate visual art into other content areas!

Art Materials

Kindergarten teachers are notorious for collecting and saving just about everything. The junk they keep often proves to be treasures for the art center!

You may want to start collecting these goodies: cardboard tubes, juice can lids, fabric scraps, feathers, little shells, yarn, wrapping-paper scraps, magazine pictures, plastic foam pieces, cotton balls, cardboard pieces, various utensils and gadgets, sticks, ribbons, socks, lace, beads, beans, pasta, strawberry baskets, paper of all shapes and textures, egg cartons, wood scraps, cat food cans, baby food jars, little yogurt containers, plastic and foil trays, cotton swabs, hangers, shoe boxes, wallpaper samples, and buttons.

Art Wish List

Many parents will want to donate items to your program, so keep a list of things they can save or buy, such as paper plates and craft items. Here is a list of basic art supplies every kindergarten classroom should have:

Tempera paint (at least one gallon of each of the primary colors, plus black and white)

white and colored construction paper (9" x 12" and 12" x 18")

watercolor sets and brushes

colored chalk or pastels

crayons

felt markers

scissors with curved ends

clear tape and masking tape

white glue

staplers

glue sticks

oak tag (plain and colored)

butcher paper

easel brushes (⅝" to 1") and easel paper

clay (pottery-type as well as plasticine)

clay tools

variety of brushes and rollers

It's also nice to have glitter, colored tissue paper, colored pencils, pipe cleaners, rubber stamps, sponge shapes, stencils, hole punchers, "wiggly eyes", stamp pads, stencils, craft sticks, felt, crepe paper, and cellophane.

Have on hand: smocks or old shirts, hangers and clothespins, paper towels, plastic cloths and place mats, trays, newspapers, starch, wax paper and string.

Some Favorite Art Activities

Painting

Offer more than brushes to paint with, including cotton swabs and cotton balls, forks, tree branches, marbles, and feathers. Paint thinned with water can be used for straw painting, and with eyedroppers and syringes. Finger paint is a very satisfying medium and encourages one part of the brain to "talk" to the other. Adding salt or glitter to paint makes lovely sparkles. Easel painting is a must for many reasons, including the fact it encourages children to work BIG and strengthens the shoulder girdle area, which helps with the task of handwriting. Paint on all types of paper and other materials! Provide paper cut into different large shapes such as ovals, triangles, diamonds, hearts, and cloud shapes. (You may have to cut your paper into these shapes.)

Children can paint on a variety of surfaces such as tree bark, glass, or even a fish (dead, of course, but fresh!). Students press a sheet of paper over the freshly-painted object, then lift the paper to reveal a print! Try a variety of textures and shapes. Have them guess what items other students used. They also can dip everyday objects and gadgets (corks, hair brushes, sponges, vegetables, leaves) into thick paint and stamp a design on paper.

Collage

There are many ways to approach this technique, including gluing "found" objects (buttons, scraps, leaves) onto paper or cardboard. Students can create collages using magazine pictures, overlapping tissue paper (use laundry starch for a shiny effect) or colored cellophane. Make fabric and paper collages using different sizes and shapes.

Old Favorites

Don't forget murals, mobiles, masks, chalk drawing on pavement, papier-mâché, dioramas, and sculpture. Remember the pleasures of simple crayon drawing and wonderful, moist clay!

> **To give a fair chance to potential creativity is a matter of life and death for any society.**
>
> —Arnold Toynbee

Music

Every kindergarten must have music every day. A classroom without music lacks the life blood that nourishes the spirit. Music plays many roles in a classroom. Children respond naturally to music, which is processed on two levels: the cognitive and the affective. When children sing, they can remember concepts more easily. They also develop an awareness of rhythm, pitch and other features of music. There is often an emotional response to music, and children are usually more relaxed after they have been singing.

Children who can't tune in to spoken words will notice the same words when carried on a melody ("We are waiting, we are waiting, for Ben to join us, on the rug."). Classical music played softly in the background can create a soothing atmosphere and encourage children to focus on their work. Research shows that some classical music, such as Bach's, helps build more neural pathways in the brain. Singing rounds like "Row, Row, Row Your Boat" can develop listening skills, enhance memory, and support children with auditory processing problems. Playing musical instruments invites children to explore sound, create their own music, and develop confidence in handling the instruments. Singing can actually change children's brain chemistry, helping them to feel more relaxed, self-confident, and able to perform on cognitive tasks.

Start off each day with music. Children love to join the singing of a favorite song, and it helps to create a feeling of unity. Include songs with body motions. This not only makes it more fun, but it gives different parts of the brain practice working together. If you don't play a musical instrument, learn how now! You don't have to be musically gifted, you just need to be willing to try. Kindergartners are very forgiving, so find something to play. Don't worry how your voice sounds, and have FUN. Guitars, keyboards, and autoharps are the easiest to learn, and it's amazing how many songs you can play with just two or three notes! At the very least, beat on a little drum or shake a maraca.

Using Music in the Classroom

- Use music in all content areas.

- Listen to a variety of music.

- Include music from different cultures.

- Paint to different kinds of music.

- Sing number songs and put science facts to music.

- Include songs in all your social studies units.

- Surround the children with enlarged print songs and chants they can read as a group or individually.

- Make class and individual songbooks.

- Use finger plays ("Where Is Thumbkin?") and songs with hand motions ("In a Cabin in the Woods," "The Wheels on the Bus," "John Brown's Baby," etc.).

39

Songs and Chants Kindergartners Love

"Get on Board" (traditional)

I have a friend that we all know, and (child) is her/his name.

I have a friend that we all know and (next child in circle) is her/his name.

Get on board, (first child) and (second child),

Get on board, (first child) and (second child),

Get on board, (first child) and (second child),

There's room for many a more!

(Keep going around the circle.)

"The More We Get Together" (tune: "Did You Ever See a Lassie?")

The more we get together, together, together,

The more we get together, the happier we'll be.

For my friends are your friends, and your friends are my friends

The more we get together, the happier we'll be!

There's (child) and (child) and (child) and (child)

(Continue until everyone's name is called. For variety, repeat the beginning lines between each group of names.)

"Name-o" (tune: "Bingo")

We have a friend in kindergarten, and (child) is her/his name-o,

(Sing and clap the letters of the child's name three times.)

And (child) was his/her name-o!

Note: As you are singing, it is helpful to hold up a sign displaying the child's name. Point to each letter as you sing it out.

"Who Stole the Cookie from the Cookie Jar?" (chant)

Who stole the cookie from the cookie jar?

(Slap thighs in rhythm during chant.)

(Child) stole the cookie from the cookie jar!

Child responds: "Who me?"

Whole class: "Yes, you!"

Child answers: "Couldn't be!"

Class: "Then who?"

Child responds by naming another child.

(Keep on repeating, giving others a turn.)

Variation: Write the words on a large chart. Cut a pocket in the shape of a cookie jar. Paste it to the chart and insert a few name cards. As you sing the song, pull a card out slowly so that a few letters are revealed. Have children guess who stole the cookie by looking at the name.

Creative Movement and Dance

Most kindergartners aren't self-conscious. They will be very responsive to your suggestions to move a certain way to music or to pretend they are something else. In fact, you'll find some children thrive on such activities!

You can find a variety of creative movement and dance activities or make up your own. They are fun to do, foster creativity and self-expression, and develop listening skills and motor coordination.

To lead these activities all you need is an imagination, a love of fun, and a good sense about how to give clear, inviting directions. Sometimes scarves, bean bags, hoops, and sticks can be useful, too.

Here are some movement ideas:

- Stomp like an elephant; creep like a mouse.

- Move around the circle in different ways such as galloping, hopping, and sliding.

- March to music. You can add instruments.

- Pretend to be a seed sprouting, and slowly growing.

- Be a balloon getting bigger, then POP!

- Have children lie on their backs and move different parts of their bodies. ("Pick up your foot. Show it the door.")

- There are good yoga postures for children they'll love to do.

- Also check out "Sammy," "The Bean Bag," and other great movement songs by Hap Palmer! And don't forget the old favorites such as "Head, Shoulders, Knees and Toes," and "If You're Happy and You Know It"!

Check It Out!

Rise Up Singing: The Group-Singing Song Book by Peter Blood-Patterson (Sing Out Publications, 1989)

Wee Sing and Play by Pamela Conn Beall and Susan Hagan Nipp (Price/Stern/Sloan, 1986)

Learning Through Play: Music & Movement by Ellen Booth Church (Scholastic, 1992)

Circle Time Activities for Young Children by Deya Brashears and Sharron Werlin Krull (DMC Publications)

Try to teach your students dances. Dance strengthens a variety of cognitive and motor skills and builds confidence! Some favorite kindergarten dances include The Farmer in the Dell, The Bunny Hop, The Hokey Pokey, and London Bridge. Kindergartners also love simple square dances, waltzes, folk dances, and Native American or African dances, as well as swaying and jumping to different types of music.

Drama

Some children are natural actors and put their whole selves into dramatizing stories and other types of characterization. Others are a bit shy or confused at times about what to do. They need lots of time and gentle encouragement. Never force a reluctant child to get in front of others and perform.

You may choose to do an "official" play, and perform it in front of parents or other classes. If so, it's best to keep it simple and meaningful, and let the children have a say in how it's done. Everyone should have a part, even if it's painting the scenery or announcing the name of the play. Everyone who wants to act should have a chance to perform, so find plays that have lots of roles or groups of people, or present more than one play.

Give the children lots of time to practice the play, and, as much as possible, involve them in collecting and making props, costumes, and scenery. Parents and older students can help as well.

A less-complicated approach to a drama performance is for the children to act out short, familiar stories. They can also act out songs, with everyone singing along. Poems can also be recited and acted out.

Remember that you will usually need to model what it is the children should do. Often big, exaggerated movements, and loud, clear "stage" voices need to be encouraged. Ham it up a bit, and allow for frequent mistakes. (Relax! People are charmed by kindergarten goofs!) You'll have a blast!

Some good stories to act out include tales such as The Three Little Pigs. Simple early reader books contain stories, such as the Joy Cowley books *One Cold Wet Night, Mrs. Wishy-Washy,* and *The Farm Concer*t (all from The Wright Group), that are fun to perform.

Puppets — Have on hand a variety of people and animal puppets, and encourage the students to make some, too. Shadow puppets are a no-mess favorite. Paper bags, socks, and cardboard can all be decorated to make interesting puppets. Buy, build or rig up a puppet theater. It's a sure hit!

Masks — You can find many ideas for mask-making in books and from art teachers. Children love masks and learn a lot in the process of creating them.

Performances — Attend shows and invite entertainers to your classroom. Students will be inspired by puppet shows, magic acts, musicals, dance performances, and plays.

> **It is the supreme art of the teacher to awaken joy in creative expression and knowledge.**
>
> —Albert Einstein

PHYSICAL DEVELOPMENT

Five- and six-year-olds are full of energy and need lots of opportunities to run, jump, and climb. Without frequent opportunities to exercise, they can become restless. As their teacher, it is your responsibility to insure that they not only get outside to let off steam, but that a variety of activities are provided to enhance their gross and fine motor development.

Structure your program so that the development of these physical skills happens naturally, within the context of daily activities. When students carry big blocks, paint at the easel, skip around the rug, and swing on the monkey bars, they are becoming stronger, more coordinated, and increasingly confident. And all of these activities encourage the muscles and brain to work together more efficiently.

You also want to provide opportunities to develop the capacity for each student's brain hemispheres to work together. Each side of the brain does important work, but each side needs the other for optimum success. When the brain hemispheres communicate effectively, reasoning skills are enhanced. Performance on a variety of physical and mental tasks are also improved. If the right and left sides of a child's brain fail to communicate effectively, the child may have motor problems, attention disorders, and language processing difficulties.

To encourage the crossing of the midline (right and left side communication), plan various motor activities, such as reaching and grabbing games, in which students must move their hands and arms from one side of their bodies to the other.

Most children of this age enjoy going to physical education class, although it might be hard for some to pay attention and follow directions! If you are lucky enough to have a gym teacher in your school, be sure to talk to him or her about what skills are being developed and how everyone is doing. Visit the PE class once in awhile. You can reinforce some of the skill development during your own large muscle activities with the children.

Large Motor Activities and Equipment

The following activities help develop large motor skills.

On the Playground: swings, monkey bars, ball play (throwing, catching, kicking), climbing structure, hopscotch, running, ring toss, sidewalk chalk drawing, basketball, jump rope (individual and group), bike riding, wagon pulling, ladder and slide, and digging in the sandbox. Traditional games like "Duck-Duck-Goose," "Mother May I?," and "Red Light, Green Light" are fun, but vary how much exercise the participants get.

Indoors: building with large hollow blocks, bean bag toss, creative movement activities (galloping, skipping, stretching), working at vertical surfaces (blackboard, easel), walking up and down stairs, balancing activities, walking on tape on rug, dancing, and jumping games.

You will find a wide range of physical abilities and levels of development. However, you may have students who stand out as having developmental weaknesses. For example, be on the alert for children who:

- stumble a lot and spill things

- run with an awkward gait

- appear very young in their movements

- seem to lack strength or flexibility in parts of their bodies

- have a lot of difficulty performing motor tasks (catching a ball, balancing on one foot, walking on tip-toes)

Discuss your concerns with your principal or school occupational or physical therapist. There may be ways to help the child with therapy, modifications in the classroom, or activities done in the home.

> **They are able because they think they are able.**
>
> —Virgil

Never Give Up Recess!

In the crunch to cover all subject areas, some administrators and teachers have opted to eliminate recess from daily schedules. However, unstructured outdoor play time is much more than "just playing." Recess is essential for the social, emotional, physical, and intellectual growth of children. On the playground, students enhance their thinking skills. Active, multi-sensory play engages the brain more fully than passive learning.

During recess, children have an opportunity to "let off steam," which can help them focus more closely on school work. Running and jumping make students more relaxed and confident as learners.

On the playground, children develop aspects of their personalities which aren't evident in the classroom. A withdrawn child can become animated, and a disruptive child can become the enthusiastic leader of a game.

Recess allows kids to get the physical exercise they need. Today's children are increasingly sedentary and overweight. Recess may be one of the few times they get to use their large muscles and work up a sweat. Good muscle development and coordination helps children with a variety of academic tasks, including writing.

During recess, children can explore the outdoors. Students can use all five senses to observe an ever-changing natural environment. Even the starkest urban play areas offer interesting outdoor textures and patterns!

Recess is a time when children practice their social skills. The playground is often the place where children learn to take turns, negotiate, and develop strategies for coping with changing friendships.

Children can also solve problems and develop feelings of autonomy on the playground. Unstructured play time offers children choices about where to go, what to do, what to use, and who to be with. Risk-taking on the playground can bolster confidence which can carry over into the classroom.

Recess offers you the opportunity to authentically assess your students. When teachers only view the "indoor child," they only know part of the child. We can learn a great deal by watching and having fun with children on the playground. Observing how children move and interact, and seeing the choices they make can tell us a lot about our students. Sometimes these observations can alert us to problems we may not have otherwise noticed.

Small Motor Activities and Materials

Before kindergartners can write with pencils or perform other fine motor tasks, they need to possess sufficient upper body strength and coordination, as well as adequate visual-motor skills. Some children enter school already writing letters and making representational drawings, while others have little experience or interest in these tasks. It is best to ease children into these activities gradually by giving them lots of choices and opportunities to practice.

Games and Manipulatives—marbles, large jacks, pick-up-sticks, lacing activities, peg boards, pop-beads, card games, Tic-Tac-Toe played on a chalk board, "cat's cradle," clothespins, tweezers, and board games that use little pieces, spinners, or tongs

Art and Crafts—bead stringing, watercolor painting, paper folding and coloring with crayons. Tearing and crumpling paper, using hole punches, playing with clay and gluing small objects to paper also develop the small muscles. Drawing on chalkboards or other vertical surfaces (especially dot-to-dot or tracing mazes) encourages the crossing of the midlines, helps strengthen fingers, and develops stability in the trunk, shoulders, and wrists.

Music—playing musical instruments (keyboard, stringed instruments)

Math—inch cubes; geoboards; buttons; pattern blocks; interlocking cubes; puzzles; and coloring, cutting, and gluing patterns and designs

Cooking—holding bowls while stirring, using egg-beaters, kneading dough, rolling dough into balls

Water Play—pouring, using spray bottles, eyedroppers, turkey basters, and pumps

Writing—tactile activities (writing in sand or shaving cream, tracing sandpaper letters), vibrating pens, molding clay (or cookie dough or pretzels) into shapes and letters and numbers,

creating rainbow letters (children trace large letters with different-colored markers or crayons)

Also—sand and water play; using zippers, snaps, and buttons; finger play; magic tricks; opening jars; turning door knobs and keys; and using blocks and other construction toys. Also, outdoor activities such as climbing ladders and swinging on monkey bars can strengthen the arm muscles. Swinging can build trunk strength and stability, which supports children's ability to do handwriting.

HANDWRITING

Because many kindergartners aren't ready to form letters on paper yet, it's best to reserve handwriting instruction for only those who are ready. If you do decide to have everyone practice letter formation, stay relaxed and watch for signs of frustration. Be sure the children's feet are secure on the floor and that the table is at a good height. The paper needs to be at a slight angle to the child's body (top tilted to the left for right-handed students, and to the right for left-handed writers). Some teachers use primary pencils, which are thicker than the standard yellow pencils. There are triangular-shaped pencils, as well as rubber pencil grips to put on pencils as needed. Consult your school's occupational therapist for guidance. Before you lead a handwriting lesson, you may want to have students do some fun hand warm-ups by making fists and stretching their fingers. Encourage a tripod pencil grasp.

Accept all the children's handwriting efforts, and use careful judgment about "correcting" what they've done. It helps to keep handwriting instruction time short, and to have the children practice on a vertical surface as much as possible before writing on paper. You can also give them dotted shapes, letters, and numbers to trace before they write independently.

When students do their journals and other writing activities, accept their writing as it is, except in those cases where you know little effort was put forth. Children who are struggling may need you to write their words, or to make dot letters for them to write over. You could also use a yellow highlighter marker to write words that students can write over.

Model the desired letter formation. When you write on a chart, or label an item in the room, print the letters the same way you want the children to write them. Make the strokes the same way they are being taught. All other adults who work in the room should do the same. (A large manuscript chart posted in the room is useful as a reference for both students and teachers!)

Keep in mind that children who aren't yet ready to write will still have a need to express themselves. Give them lots of opportunities to dictate their words to you. Those who have some phonemic awareness can type their ideas on a computer or typewriter, if holding a pencil is too frustrating for them. As the months go by and their hands strengthen, you can encourage some writing and see how it goes.

On the next page is a manuscript guide. Check that these guidelines match your school's style. Some teachers mount these guides on colored tag board and laminate them. Included on the page is a name-writing guide that each student can use at home as well.

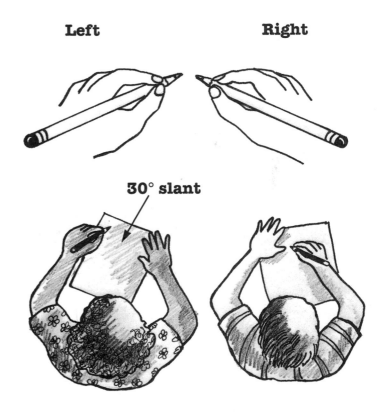

Left   **Right**

30° slant

Name _____

MANUSCRIPT ALPHABET

Aa Bb Cc Dd Ee Ff

Gg Hh Ii Jj Kk Ll

Mm Nn Oo Pp Qq Rr

Ss Tt Uu Vv Ww Xx

Yy Zz

Here's how I'm learning to write my name in school.

_____

- -

_____

- -

_____

Can you help me practice at home?

48
reproducible

FS122002 Getting Ready to Teach Kindergarten

> **Be true to your teeth, then they'll never be false to you.**
>
> —Soupy Sales

HEALTH

Kindergartners are old enough to have a good understanding of basic health and safety concepts. They are receptive to guidance about how to take care of their bodies and will be willing and able to do the following:

- wash and dry their hands after toileting, coughing, or blowing their noses, and before eating, cooking, or using the water table

- cover their noses and mouths when sneezing or coughing and wash their hands afterwards

- use tissue to blow their noses

- avoid sharing cups, straws, and other items that spread germs

- wear appropriate attire, such as raincoats, jackets, or boots (Parent cooperation is useful here!)

Your students will enjoy activities related to healthy eating and dental care, so consider including these in your curriculum. Prepare healthy snacks and encourage nutritious snacks from home. Invite your school nurse to visit to talk about health issues, such as how to properly brush teeth or prevent the spread of head lice. You may need to tell your students not to touch each other's blood.

SAFETY

Safety education is an ongoing process in kindergarten. Teachers must be aware of what their students are doing at all times, and redirect any unsafe behavior. The safe behavior you'll want to develop in your students includes:

- walking in the classroom

- using scissors, hammers, and other tools carefully

- using chairs or tables correctly

- keeping sand and water in appropriate locations

- walking carefully with sticks, scissors, pencils, and other pointed objects

- creating sturdy block structures and "unbuilding" them safely

- observing stop signs, rules, and boundaries during recess, on field trips, and on the bus

- treating others with gentleness and respect

Provide the children with additional safety information, some of which relates to the home. Fire prevention awareness is highly important, as is knowing emergency procedures such as how to evacuate the school or their homes and what telephone number to call. At Halloween time, discuss basic safety rules pertaining to costumes, traffic, and treats. Personal safety issues related to strangers and abuse are important, but discuss this with your school principal and guidance counselor first, as this is a sensitive subject for many. Keep in mind that police and fire departments, as well as utility companies, often send people to schools to lead safety programs.

As with other subjects in kindergarten, do not assume that your students know basic health and safety practices. You just might be the first one who shows a child how to wash his or her hands!

COMPUTERS

If you have access to a computer in your classroom, there are ways it can be used appropriately. But before you decide how to utilize the computer, ask yourself the following questions:

- In what ways will using the computer help my students grow and develop?

- How and when will the computer be used?

- Will an adult need to be with the computer user(s)?

- How much classroom space will it need? (Perhaps your students will go to a computer lab.)

- Will the sounds from the computer be a distraction to others?

- Will the sounds from the classroom interfere with hearing the computer?

- Is the available software appropriate and meaningful for five-year-olds?

- Are the programs process-oriented? Are the problems open-ended?

If you teach a full-day kindergarten, it will be easier for you to accommodate a computer in your classroom. It can be used it to create stories and art, especially if you have access to a printer. Some excellent software programs

are available, and you can find out what's good by asking other teachers, librarians, friends, and parents. Choose software that allows children to be as creative as possible. If you're not comfortable with computers, find a friend, parent, or teacher to help you.

Use computers to enhance the learning that's already taking place. Reading and math skills can be reinforced with computers.

Pair students to use the computer together. Working together helps them to practice their communication and cooperation skills. Perhaps you have some experienced computer users who can be your "experts." Also consider getting help from older students.

If you have just a few hours a day with students or are on a limited budget, don't feel guilty about not scheduling computer time. Always keep in mind that kindergartners need to be interacting with each other and you.

Check It Out!

Failure To Connect—How Computers Affect Our Children's Minds—For Better or Worse by Jane M. Healy, Ph.D. (Simon & Schuster, 1998).

Software: *Thinkin' Things—Collection 1* (Edmark) and *The Ultimate Writing and Creativity Center* (The Learning Company)

CARPENTRY

Working with wood can be very satisfying for children. The feel and the smell of lumber gives pleasure, as does the successful pounding of a nail through wood. If your budget can afford it, purchase some woodworking equipment and supplies for your classroom. Since you don't need to do carpentry all the time, you can purchase and share the supplies with several teachers. It will be money well spent!

Here's what you'll need:

- a carpenter's bench (woodworking table)

- a vise, especially if you plan to allow sawing

- two hammers (child-sized, yet sturdy)

- safety goggles

- an assortment of nails

- wood glue

- sandpaper

- hand saw (optional)

- also optional: screwdrivers, hand drill, clamps, pliers

- wood scraps (You can get these from lumber yards, building sites, and/or carpenter friends. Soft pine is best. Keep away from rough, splintery wood or pressure-treated wood.)

TIP!

A piece of carpet on your woodworking table will help to reduce the noise in your classroom.

If you aren't familiar with carpentry yourself, take some time to practice using the tools. Find some books on carpentry for children so you'll know the best methods of instruction as well as safety guidelines. Invite a carpenter to visit the classroom to help the children with a simple project.

Here are some other tips for making carpentry fun and safe:

- Have your woodworking area in the "noisy" part of the room or in an outdoor area.

- Children must be supervised. Limit the number of children at the center—two is best. Require goggles at all times, and give careful instructions regarding appropriate handling of the tools.

- Allow woodworking during active free choice times.

- Remove children who are endangering themselves or others.

- Rotate children through the carpentry area so that everyone gets a turn.

- Integrate carpentry with other content areas. Make cars and airplanes during a unit on transportation, boats for your water unit, planter boxes for Mother's Day, or houses during your study of shelters.

- Offer paint, sequins, bottle caps, yarn, and other items for decorating wood projects. Use the art center for this stage of the process.

51

> Food is our common ground, a universal experience.
>
> —James Beard, Beard on Food, 1974

COOKING

Perhaps nothing engenders more enthusiasm from children than food and the prospect of consuming it. It can be hard to find time for cooking projects, but try to do them at least once a week. If you are responsible for providing a daily snack for your students, the children will enjoy preparing it. Not only are cooking and eating extremely pleasurable, but they have many inherent learning opportunities.

For example, science concepts are explored as students mix water with oil, dry ingredients with wet ones, study the contents of an egg, and watch what heat does to dough.

A variety of math concepts are learned and reinforced as students count out teaspoons, measure cups of water, set the timer, and try to figure out if two dozen muffins will be enough to feed the class.

Reading skills are reinforced as children read enlarged-print, illustrated recipes. Literature-inspired meals abound, such as "Stone Soup." Food lends itself well to multicultural exploration in the form of quesadillas, potato latkes, or tempura.

Make friends with your school cook, if you have one! If you don't have access to a conventional oven consider getting a large toaster oven. A hot plate also can be useful for stove-top recipes, such as soup, pancakes, and scrambled eggs. An electric frying pan can be useful as well. In any case, check with your principal or custodian before using heavy-duty appliances, and always keep the children's safety your number-one priority!

Some Tips for Providing Successful Cooking Activities

- Choose your recipes carefully. Keep them simple, and bear in mind what types of food children enjoy.

- Be aware of any food allergies among your students.

- Make a big, illustrated copy of the recipe for your cooks to read along with you.

- Be prepared by having everything ready to use.

- Keep the group size manageable (3–6 children is best).

- Make sure the children wash their hands first (and re-wash after their little tasting fingers go into their mouths!).

- Talk about the recipe first, allowing the children to offer their ideas about it.

- Explore the ingredients: feel the soft flour; smell the cinnamon and vanilla.

- Make sure everyone has a turn to do something (measure one teaspoon of salt, stir 10 times, mash one banana, pour the oil).

- Ask cooks to make predictions about what will happen when the egg gets beaten, the milk gets added, the potato boils, or the cheese gets hot.

- Have the cooks help with cleaning up. It's all part of the process!

Some favorite cooking projects include cookies (chocolate chip, oatmeal), bread (whole wheat, banana), pizza, pancakes, pretzels, pudding, butter, soups, scrambled eggs, gingerbread people, muffins, ants-on-a-log (peanut butter on celery dotted with raisins), grilled cheese, nachos, flavored ice, hot cereal, smoothies, and applesauce.

> **We become not a melting pot but a beautiful mosaic. Different people, different beliefs, different yearnings, different hopes, different dreams.**
>
> **—Jimmy Carter, speech, Pittsburgh, Pennsylvania, October 27, 1976**

MULTICULTURALISM

All children need help in developing their awareness of, and respect for, people of all ethnicities, beliefs, and abilities. Embed multiculturalism in your curriculum. Reflect it in the activities you provide, the language you use, the books you select, and the materials you offer.

Some teachers tend to view multiculturalism as a tourist would, by "visiting" various cultures through sampling their food and admiring their "costumes." However, young children will feel a greater connection with others when they learn of the similarities between them. For example:

- Present a unit on bread. Children can learn how breads are made and used around the world. Discover the different types of bread enjoyed by their classmates, such as bagels, pita, chapati, and tortillas.

- Study shelters around the world, including the homes of your students. This leads nicely into learning about weather, geography, building materials, etc.

- Include various cultures in units of study. For example, a unit on night could include lullabies from around the world.

- Focus on holidays that people have in common, such as harvest celebrations and festivals of light.

- Read stories about children of all ethnicities and abilities. Include folk tales and fairy tales from different cultures.

- Invite visitors to your classroom who will help you with your goal of bridging cultural gaps and dispelling stereotypes. Find a female carpenter to help with your woodworking. Invite a Native American (in "regular" clothes) to come in to read a story. If you know someone in a wheelchair, perhaps he or she can do a project with the children.

Keep your program as bias-free as possible. Young children are already forming perceptions about skin color, gender, and power. Be sure your books, puzzles, dolls, and posters show a variety of people in honest, non-stereotypical ways. Watch your language for subtle signs of discrimination. For example, avoid telling your students to sit "Indian-style." Resist asking for "strong boys" as volunteers, or lining up students by gender. Even asking children what their mothers cooked for dinner sends a message that only women are the family cooks. Watch for your assumptions. Not all kids have two parents at home. Not everyone celebrates birthdays and Easter. Enjoy the journey of discovery as you celebrate and honor our human race!

Check It out!

Anti-Bias Curriculum by Louise Derman-Sparks and the A.B.C. Task Force (NAEYC, 1989).

Children Just Like Me by Barnabas and Anabel Kindersley (DK Publishing, 1995).

Teaching Tolerance, published twice a year by the Southern Poverty Law Center, 400 Washington Avenue, Montgomery AL, 36104.

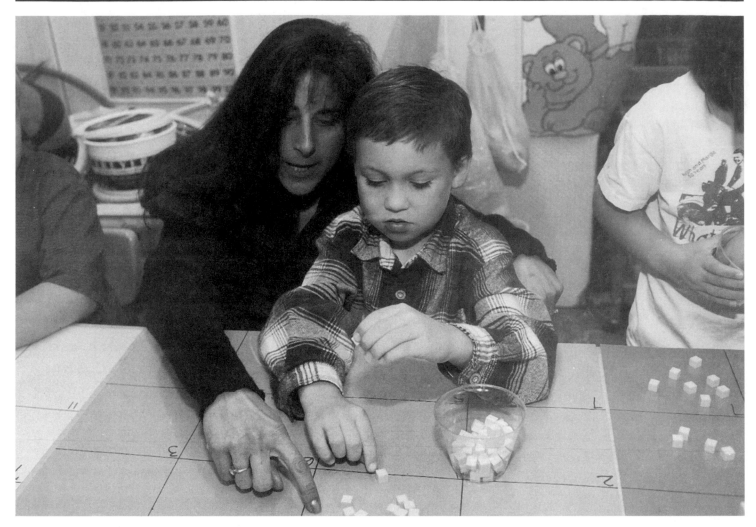

CHAPTER THREE: THE CLASSROOM

PUTTING IT ALL TOGETHER

Okay, now that you've been introduced to curriculum areas, how in the world do you put it all together? This will be one of the biggest challenges you face. But don't despair! There are ways.

First of all, realize you need to make some hard choices. You can't always do everything, and no one is expecting you to. If you have a half-day program and your children have gym, library, art, and other "specials," the opportunities for classroom learning are pretty limited. If you live

where it snows, much of your time will be taken up with putting on and taking off winter apparel, leaving you with perhaps an hour of teaching time during that season!

So decide what's most important for your students, keeping in mind what's developmentally appropriate, and do your best to provide those learning experiences.

Making It Work

Use Learning Centers

When you have math, writing, science, listening, art, and block centers in your classroom, as well as a book corner, sand and water table, and drama area, you are setting up your room for maximum learning potential in all the curriculum areas.

Provide Choices

Make a schedule that provides for a balance of free choice and "must-do's." A must-do is an activity which you require students to participate in. A must-do can be anything from placing children in a learning center they've never been in to asking them to join you for a game of number bingo. Must-do's are one way of insuring that all children are developing in the areas you feel are important.

Combine Content Areas

Integrate your activities as much as possible. It not only makes the experiences more meaningful for the children, but it gives you the opportunity to incorporate more skills and concepts within fewer activities. For example, instead of having a whole-class, daily language arts time, you can teach important concepts about print during your morning message, help children make signs for their block constructions, and have them dictate their science predictions while you write their ideas and read them back. You probably can't do a half-hour of math a day, but you can incorporate it into just about every activity that you do provide.

SCHEDULING

Many variables are involved when creating a schedule, some of them beyond your control. Some kindergartens have a set recess time, as well as times to go to "specials." You might have speech therapists or paraprofessionals scheduled to work in your room at specific times. Trying to find the right time to do extended learning activities can be a real headache! Here are some ideas to help you:

1. Be as flexible as possible.

2. Try to coordinate schedules ahead of time. Talk to those people who work with your students. Enlist the help of your principal.

3. Keep transitions to a minimum.

4. Get copies of other kindergarten schedules.

5. Have a regular, predictable weekly schedule. Kindergartners need this structure. Parents appreciate it, too.

6. Check your schedule to see if it allows for a balance of activities (free choice/must-do's, small/large group, active/quiet).

7. Give your schedule a chance to succeed before changing it.

8. If adjustments must be made, make them. Let the children know ahead of time if possible.

9. Don't expect it all to be perfect.

10. Keep your sense of humor!

Use the sample schedules on pages 56 and 57 as references when you create a class schedule of your own.

> **We should establish classrooms where children are encouraged to take responsibility for their learning, to become independent writers, readers, thinkers, and speakers, and to take an active role in creating a more just society.**
>
> **—Michael Hartoonian**

TWO HALF-DAY SCHEDULES

"Ms. A's" Schedule

8:30	Arrival — Children greeted, settle in. Small motor work at tables (clay, drawing, puzzles, board games, pattern blocks, etc.).
9:00	Morning Meeting — Song, greeting, attendance, milk count, morning message, sharing, game or story, plans for the morning. On Mondays explain new centers and "must-do's." Children choose new jobs.
9:30	Choice Time — Children work in different centers. When aide and volunteers are available, Ms. A. does some small group instruction for part of this time.
10:20	Clean-up
10:30	Story (shared reading or read aloud)
10:45	Snack and recess
11:15	Good-bye Circle — Review the day, song, pass out notes, etc.
11:30	Dismissal

"Mr. B's" Schedule

8:30	Arrival — Children greeted, settle in, answer the "daily question" (graph, prediction, science mystery guess, draw picture on chart from field trip, etc.). Journals, free reading around the room.
9:00	Welcome Circle — Song, friendly greeting, morning message, "daily question" answers shared, calendar, attendance, plan for morning.
9:30	Work Time — Children work in centers, some are with Mr. B for a "must-do."
10:00	Snack is available now for children who wish to eat.
10:30	Clean-up
10:40	Special (library, art, P.E., music)
11:00	Recess
11:15	Good-bye Circle — Story, good-byes
11:30	Dismissal

NOTE: Ms. A. teaches two half-day kindergarten classes and repeats her schedule in the afternoon. Mr. B. shares a classroom with another teacher and helps her in the afternoon when her class is in session.

FULL-DAY SCHEDULE

"Mrs. C's Schedule"

	Monday	Tuesday	Wednesday	Thursday	Friday
8:30	Welcome: Journals and Free Reading	Welcome: Table Time (small motor activities)	Welcome: Table Time	Welcome: Table Time	Welcome: Table Time
9:00	Morning Meeting: Song, Game, Attendance, Milk Count, Calendar, Greeting, Sharing Plan for Day				
9:30	Big Workshop (Choice Time)	Big Workshop	Big Workshop	Big Workshop	Library and Writing Workshop (half class at a time)
10:30	Clean-up				
10:40	Recess				
11:10	Literacy Focus: Shared Reading, Read Aloud, Interactive Writing, etc.				
11:40	Clean-up wash hands				
11:50	Lunch				
12:15	Quiet Time (rest to soft music, taped stories, etc.)				
12:45	Math (stations, tubs, games, etc.)				
1:15	Clean-up				
1:20	Gym	Art	Gym	Computer Lab	Music
1:50	Little Workshop (special project such as science, drama, social studies, etc.)				
2:20	Clean-up				
2:25	Recess				
2:45	Good-Bye Circle				
3:00	Dismissal				

NOTE: Big Workshop is the main work period of the day, with most of the learning centers open. Children choose their activities but are responsible for "must-do's" as well. An aide and parent volunteers help. A second recess is scheduled before dismissal (not after lunch) because of the cold winters, and Mrs. C. wants to reduce the number of times children get in and out of snowsuits!

EQUIPMENT AND MATERIALS

You may be entering a classroom that is fully equipped with beautiful oak furniture, shiny new tea sets, and colorful pattern blocks. Or, like many teachers, you have may inherited a well-worn room containing a variety of mismatched furniture and toys in need of a bit of paint or glue. Whether you have a big budget or a small one, there are ways to get much of what you need to offer a quality program for kindergartners. Here is a list of what you'll need for your kindergarten program.

Furniture and Equipment

You'll need enough strong tables and chairs (five- and six-year-old size) to accommodate your class, plus sturdy shelves for books, games, and learning center materials. For the drama area you may want to supply a play stove, sink and refrigerator, doll bed and little table with chairs, mirror, clothes rack, or other storage. Some comfy chairs or cushions are good in the book area. The art area needs one or two painting easels and a drying rack or shelf. Other furniture needed are a sand/water table and an easel for big books and chart paper. Other equipment includes a hot plate, record player and/or tape player, listening center jack box, headphones, and playground items such as balls, jump ropes, and a structure for climbing.

General Materials

Teacher supplies — bins and tubs for storage, file folders, labels, stationery, note cards, envelopes (small and large manila), a plan book, a calendar, paper clips, metal loose-leaf rings, pens, pencils, permanent markers, a pencil sharpener, correction fluid, a stapler, staples, staple remover, rubber cement, stickers, aspirin, a bell, a timer, copy paper, sentence strips, index cards, removable notes, clipboards, adult scissors, yardstick/meterstick, ruler, hand lotion, extra shoes or boots for outdoors, an extra sweater, toothbrush and toothpaste, camera and film, blank cassette tapes, a dictionary, and plenty of replacement batteries.

First-aid box — Bandages, tweezers, cotton balls, and antiseptic. Check with your school nurse for your school's first aid guidelines.

General classroom supplies — tissues, waste baskets, sponges, hand soap, paper towels, cleanser, window cleaner, bleach (one drop in water makes a good disinfectant for dishes, table washing, and the water table), dish towels, rags, clothespins, wire or string for hanging items from ceiling (consult custodian), easel clips, safety pins, straight pins, book tape, rubber bands, flashlight, transistor radio, tacks and other items for mounting charts, bulletin board trim, clear contact paper, paper and plastic cups and plates, utensils, pitchers, napkins, dish soap, pot scrubbers, flower vases, indoor/outdoor thermometer, plastic trash bags, brooms and dust pans, newspapers, paper grocery bags, resealable plastic bags, and small plastic containers. Don't forget snack foods for hungry kids (graham crackers, pretzels), extra children's underwear, socks, and pants in case of toileting accidents, and extra boots, hats, and snowsuits.

> I've come to the frightening conclusion that I am the decisive element in the classroom. My personal approach creates the climate. My daily mood makes the weather. As a teacher, I possess a tremendous power to make a child's life miserable or joyous. I can be a tool of torture or an instrument of inspiration. I can humiliate, humor, hurt, or heal. In all situations, it is my response that decides whether a crisis will be escalated or de-escalated, a child humanized or dehumanized.
>
> —Haim Ginott

Learning Center Materials

Science center — magnifying glasses (large tripod kind as well as small hand-held ones), microscope (pocket illuminated 30X is good, as are the primary plastic kind), and a balance scale. More items are listed in the "Scientific Thinking" section found on page 30.

Math — Number charts, numeral writing cards, sorting hoops, tubs of wooden pattern blocks, plastic cubes and rods, color tiles, attribute blocks, and a variety of items to sort and count. Also include balance scales, rulers, games, calculators, primary number cards, geoboards and colorful rubber bands, playing cards, pattern block stamps, stamp pads, and a number pocket chart.

Block area — large set of hard wooden blocks, assorted toy vehicles, hard hats, plastic people figures (realistic and of various ethnicities and abilities), plastic farm and wild animals, wooden furniture, carpet and fabric pieces, pulleys, and items for signs (such as paper, wire, plasticine, and clothespins). Large hollow blocks and planks are good if you have the space in or out of doors. A steering wheel mounted on wood is also popular.

Drama corner — variety of hats, shoes, purses, and dress-up clothes; a telephone; various fire station and hospital props; puppets; baby dolls of different races; baby clothes; pots and pans; dishes; utensils; groceries; and multicultural plastic food. Also include office supplies such as clipboards, telephone books, appointment books, a typewriter, and a calculator.

Sand/water table — sand/water wheels, pump, plastic tubes, funnels, colander, toy boats, cups, buckets, shovels, dishes, spoons, spray bottles, and clean sand.

Art center — plastic cloth, trays, place mats or boards for clay work, paint cups, assorted brushes, and tubs and boxes for supplies. More items are listed in the "Art" section found on pages 37 and 38.

Music area — records and tapes of all kinds of music and instruments. Please see the "Music" section found on page 39.

Listening center — two to four headphones attached to a tape player, book and tape sets (two to four hard copies of the recorded story), and music tapes.

Writing center — small chalkboards, plain and lined paper, assorted pencils, crayons, pens and markers, stapler, tape dispenser, date stamp and stamp pad, scissors, colored pencils, envelopes, ABC books and chart, picture dictionary, ABC stencils, cards, and stamps.

Book corner or library — labeled baskets or tubs of ABC books, nursery rhymes and poetry, number books, animal stories, folk tales, and other books. Organize by theme or topic.

Game shelf — checkers, bingo, board games, dominoes, and others your students may find interesting.

Floor toys — floor puzzles and building sets.

Meeting/movement area — bean bags, scarves, squishy ball, pointer, chart paper, markers, removable notes, musical instruments, music tapes, and records.

> ### TIP!
>
> *Make "kid pins" by writing each child's name on a wooden clothes pin. They are useful for placing names on job charts as well as on certain kinds of graphs.*

> **Every child should have mudpies, grasshoppers, waterbugs, tadpoles, frogs, mud turtles, elderberries, wild strawberries, acorns, chestnuts, trees to climb, animals to pet, hay fields, pinecones, rocks to roll, sand, snakes, huckleberries and hornets—and any child who has been deprived of these has been deprived of the best part of his education.**
> —Luther Burbank

Cooking corner—muffin tins, large and small mixing bowls, wooden spoon, rolling pins, measuring cups and spoons, grater, peelers, cutting board, masher, can opener, bottle opener, egg beater, spatula, ladle, cake pan, pie pan, cookie sheets, pizza pan, pizza cutter, pot holders, serving trays, wax paper, and aluminum foil. Basic ingredients: flour, salt, sugar, baking powder, baking soda, food coloring, and cornstarch.

Also useful—work bins or cubby shelf for children's papers and supplies, rocking chair, building toy table, dollhouse, puppet theater, overhead projector, and woodworking table and tools. Students may need a little tent or other "alone" area, while you might need a teacher's desk or table, file cabinet, and a secure cupboard for cleaning products. A class pet and pet items (cage, food, shavings), plants, an aquarium, and small refrigerator are also handy items.

SETTING UP YOUR CLASSROOM

A classroom to a teacher is like a canvas to an artist. It is during your classroom set-up that you consider space, form, color, texture, light, and movement. You are creating a physical world that must please the senses as well as be conducive to learning. The way you arrange your classroom will affect your teaching in many ways. It is well worth the effort to spend the time and energy to make your room safe, clean, cheerful, organized, and inviting to your five-year-old learners. There is no one "correct" way to set up your room, and as the weeks go by you will learn what works and what needs changing.

A good place to start is to study your space. Find out where the electrical outlets are. Consider where the sink, doors, and windows are located. These are some of the features that will influence where you put your learning centers.

Next, decide what kinds of activities and learning centers you want to have. You may want to make a list. Look over all the furniture and equipment and see what you can use for which areas. If you can't find what you need, ask other teachers and your principal or custodian. There may be shelves and other items that aren't being used.

Before you begin to push furniture around, you may want to sketch out a plan on paper. A sample floor plan can be found on page 61. Some teachers cut out paper shapes of the furniture and equipment and move them around the paper. The next step is to set things up. The only way to tell if it all works well together is to try it! Chances are you'll keep rearranging things until it feels right, so put on some music and enjoy the process.

Guidelines for Setting Up Your Classroom

- Visit other early childhood classrooms to see how they're set up. You're bound to get some great ideas!

- Consider the quality of light in the room. Is there adequate natural light? Do you need to supplement fluorescent lighting with full-spectrum light? Plan to add mirrors and other items that reflect light in different ways.

- Study the colors and textures in the classroom. Are they inviting and soothing? Plan to have a cozy area with soft pillows somewhere.

- Consider how sounds will carry in the room. If it seems the classroom will be noisy, consider placing soft materials around the room (curtains, wall coverings, carpets) for sound absorption.

- Investigate the quality of your furniture and equipment and the general surroundings. See if it's okay to add a fresh coat of paint where needed and to mend worn or shabby equipment if your budget will extend to this. School custodians and even parent volunteers can help with this.

- Plants, a quiet pet, and a softly bubbling aquarium or fountain can help create a soothing and inviting atmosphere.

- Notice how the classroom smells. Is there a musty or moldy smell? Are there curtains, heaters, and vents that need cleaning?

- Consider adding calming fragrances to the room, such as sachets or potpourris. Some teachers simmer potpourri in the classroom to relax their students.

- Be aware that some students may have allergies. Consider this when setting up your classroom, as some children are allergic to wool, dust, perfumes, fur, and various foods and chemicals.

- Leave a large space for your meeting area. Ideally, it should be able to accommodate all your students in one circle so that they face each other.

- Make sure there are pathways around the room.

- Avoid having too much furniture, which can make the room feel crowded.

- Make sure everything is at a five-year-old's level.

- Allow for maximum supervision by not obstructing your view of the room with tall shelves.

- Place your centers according to what the needs are for those activities. Science is usually best by a window. Art, water, and sand should be near a sink. The listening center, computer, and record player need outlets.

- Allow ample room for block building, and be sure the space is covered with a smooth rug.

- Place compatible centers near each other, such as writing, computer, and listening near the book area. Blocks and dramatic play can go together, as can art, and sand and water. Keep the noisiest activities away from the quietest.

- Put some thought into where your desk should go (if you want one), how and where you'll store supplies and other items, and where children's artwork and other projects should be put to dry.

- Know that you don't have to have everything available at the same time. The average-sized classroom, for example, can't accommodate every learning center, including a doll house, woodworking corner, puppet theater, sand table and water table. Usually you rotate these centers.

- Make sure each child has some kind of cubby for hanging coats and storing personal possessions.

- Get down on your hands and knees and crawl around your classroom. How does it look?

TIP!

Make your own play-dough by heating and stirring 2 cups flour, 1 cup salt, 1 tsp. cream of tartar, 2 tbsp. oil and 2 cups water with food coloring. After mixture has thickened, remove from pan, knead, and store in plastic tub or bag.

61

SAMPLE FLOOR PLAN

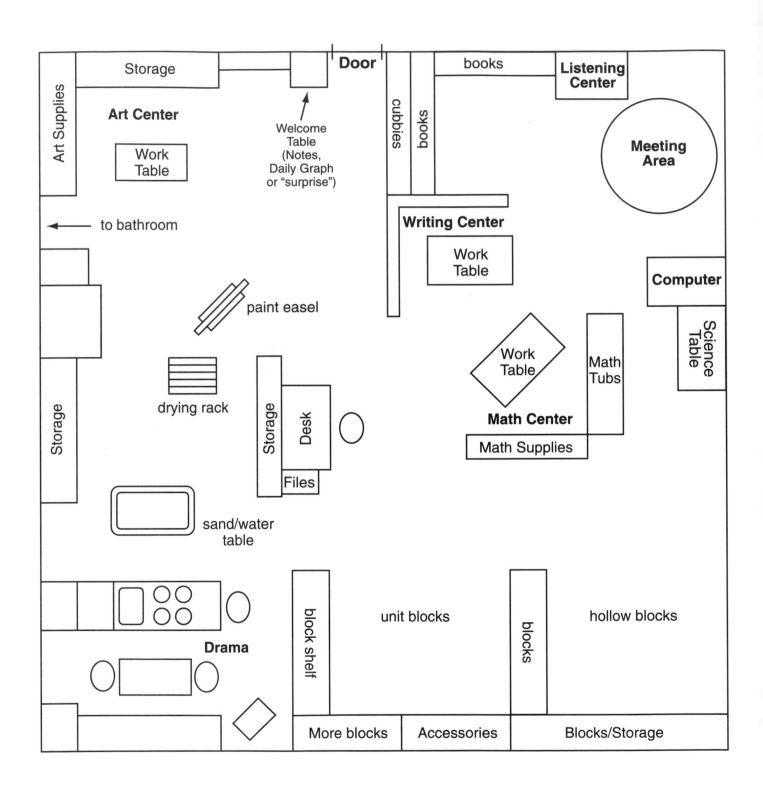

Storage

Door

books

Listening Center

Art Supplies

Art Center

Work Table

Welcome Table (Notes, Daily Graph or "surprise")

cubbies

books

Meeting Area

← to bathroom

Writing Center

Work Table

paint easel

Computer

Science Table

Work Table

Math Tubs

drying rack

Storage

Storage

Desk

Math Center

Math Supplies

Files

sand/water table

block shelf

unit blocks

blocks

hollow blocks

Drama

More blocks

Accessories

Blocks/Storage

> **Teachers are expected to reach unattainable goals with inadequate tools. The miracle is that at times they accomplish this impossible task.**
>
> —Haim G. Ginott, <u>Teacher and Child</u>, 1972

WHERE TO FIND WHAT YOU NEED

Kindergarten teachers are among the world's best scroungers. They can spot a bargain a mile away and will seize an opportunity without hesitation.

Local Shops

Beg at your local merchants. Most store managers will be happy to give you plastic trays, bird seed, and all sorts of items if you tell them you need it for your kindergarten students.

Yard Sales

Scout yard sales. Find these by looking in the newspaper, reading fliers, and keeping your eyes open for neighborhood signs. You can find true bargains for all your learning centers. You might even find some good furniture.

Discount Shops

Dollar shops and flea markets usually have sections where you can get good plastic items such as trays, baskets, and other containers. There are often other bargains, including fabric, paper, costumes, and craft items. Thrift stores are some of the best places for items for your drama area.

School Storage

Snoop around other parts of the school. You may be surprised to find just the shelf or table you need in a storage room or closet. Become friends with the custodian, and she or he will be glad to help you out.

Vacation Shopping

Vacation shopping is good. When you're in a souvenir store, museum shop, or in different geographical area, you can pick up great stuff for your science and social studies units. If you're in another country, be sure to bring back coins, postcards, and other items for school.

Friends and Neighbors

Granny's attic always has treasures, so if you know any older folks who want to reduce their attic and garage clutter, offer to help.

Retired teachers are also great resources. They have supplies, books, picture files, and other items they would be happy to pass on.

Members of your community, including your students' parents, can also help you find items. Some may donate materials to you, while others may raise money.

Your school PTA or PTO can be a great support. If you have a need, maybe they can help!

Libraries, Museums, and Universities

Libraries can be an excellent resource. Look into their books, tapes, and records. Make friends with your school librarian and local town librarian. Let them know what your upcoming topics are— they may have some ideas for you. Many materials can be acquired through interlibrary loans.

Museums, nature centers, and universities have many resources, including visiting centers, learning kits, lending libraries, and specialists who can help you.

Specialty Sources

Teacher supply stores have some excellent items. Toy stores occasionally have bargains.

Collect catalogs and scrutinize them for cost comparison. Some companies are more affordable than others. Ask other teachers and your school secretaries for ideas. You could also try asking a catalog company for a discount for your school. Some do give them.

Fund Raising

Consider fund raising. With the parents and community helping you, you might be able to get the money you need for that climbing structure or block set.

Corporate donations are another way teachers have acquired supplies. Some companies have built playgrounds and donated computers!

Closeouts and Castaways

Factory extras or rejects can be real treasures. Find out which places have "take-away" bins behind their buildings. Teachers have been known to get carloads of paper, cardboard, and other items this way.

Store closings are another opportunity to acquire classroom necessities. Don't be afraid to ask if they still need those bins and shelves!

Recycling centers sometimes have great items for your science and art centers. Some towns have "recycle for children" areas with wonderful treasures.

The outdoors is one of the best "shopping" places for science materials. Whether you're in your yard, at the beach, or meandering through the woods, always keep an eye open for an interesting feather, rock, or seed pod.

Remember to Share!

Pool resources with other teachers. Consider taking turns with the interlocking block table, puppet theater, woodworking table, etc.

> **Every journey begins with a single step.**

THE BIG DAY

Getting Ready for the First Day of School

If you have a class list before the school year begins, send a letter to each of your students. The time you spend will reap great benefits! Your students will be thrilled to get a personal letter from you, and it will help calm their first-day jitters. To save time you can photocopy the letters, but be sure to handwrite each child's name and personally sign your name. Include a few exciting tidbits about what they can expect on the first day (for example, seashells from your vacation, a mystery pet, or new trucks). A little sticker will brighten the letter. If the children need to bring something on the first day, you can mention that as well.

If you need to send a letter to the parents and are on a limited budget, you can include that information in the envelope (addressed to the child, of course) to save time and postage. Some school secretaries are happy to address and mail out these letters if they have time and are asked with great politeness. Another item you could include in the letter is a name tag which has the child's bus number and your classroom number. This can be useful if you're in a large school with many kindergartens and school buses.

You may want to send the parents a "child information questionnaire" to complete and return. This can provide you with useful information that could be handy on the first day of school. You may want to copy the sample on page 94.

There are many other things to do in order to get ready for The Big Day. The following is a partial list.

Meet with your aide and other colleagues to discuss schedules, duties, ideas, and special concerns.

Collect all necessary information from your principal, such as bus lists, special schedules, or concerns about particular students.

Read through the student files, including registration papers, developmental questionnaires, preschool records, and screening results.

Make sure you know about students' allergies and other physical problems.

Plan your snack program. (Do children bring their own snack each day? Do parents take turns sending in a class snack for everyone?)

Send your students' parents information about your program, including hours, schedule, snack and lunch needs, clothing requirements (gym days, etc.), program philosophy, and goals.

Find out where the buses arrive, and how your children will be greeted and led to the room.

Learn procedures for illnesses and accidents, plus where your students' emergency information is kept.

Take a tour of the school to learn where all the specials are held and where the supplies, including classroom materials and cleaning products, are stored.

Introduce yourself to the school staff, including the cooks, bus drivers, custodians, and nurse.

Explore the playground and other areas where your children will be.

Visit the cafeteria to learn the procedure for getting food and cleaning up.

Read through staff handbooks and district curriculum guides.

Organize your room by labeling shelves and marking centers so that students will find things with ease.

Make name tags and put names on cubbies and other personal areas.

Plan your activities for the first day, including practicing any songs.

Make sure supplies are within reach. Fill paint cups, make charts and calendars, and generally make sure everything you'll need is ready to go.

Make your classroom cheerful and welcoming by posting students' names on the door or a bulletin board display.

Find out where to go for fire drills.

Place a few attractive posters around the room, preferably of real children of different ethnicities and abilities.

Decide which areas of the room will be open to the children.

Close off areas that aren't open yet (such as blocks, as children need an introduction first). Large paper coverings, or masking tape X's work well for this purpose.

Display photographs, if available, from when the children came for Visiting Day.

Make sure there's food available for children who need it.

Find the time to relax and rest.

First Day Tips

Even the most seasoned teachers experience some anxiety about the first day of school. If you're feeling apprehensive, it's totally understandable. But as long as your room looks good and you feel prepared for at least the first day, you will do fine! Monitor your body and voice for signs of tension throughout the day, and take it slowly. Have a teacher "buddy" who can help you out as needed, whether for comfort or advice. And keep that sense of humor at all times!

- Be as rested and relaxed as possible. Take a lot of deep breaths and smile!

- Greet the students at the driveway, doorway, or wherever they come in.

- Kneel down at their level. Use their names.

- Greet the parents and let them stay until they're comfortable.

- Be sure to find out how each child goes home. Some go to an after-school program, some get picked up by parents or grandparents, some go on a different bus to a sitter.

- Let the children and parents explore the room.

- Have a few simple, soothing activities available, such as play dough, puzzles, books, and drawing. As much as possible, make these free-choice activities.

- Stay with and comfort upset or tentative children.

- Gather the children on the rug for a fun song and maybe a short story.

- Play a game or sing a song that introduces everyone.

- Tell the children what to expect from the day.

- Show them the basics of the room, including the sink, bathroom, and drinking fountain.

- Maintain a gentle, slow-paced atmosphere. If possible, avoid "specials" on the first day. Also, reserve the school tour until the second or third day, when students are feeling more comfortable.

- Interact with each child. Observe them carefully, and notice how they approach activities. Take notes when you can.

- One enjoyable activity is to have willing students produce self-portraits or other kinds of "writing" samples which are saved for the year.

THE FIRST WEEKS OF SCHOOL

The first weeks of school are your most important weeks, because it is during this time that you set the tone for the entire year. This is the time when routines are established, rules are created, and materials are gradually introduced. Your students get a feel for who you are and what to expect from you. They get to know each other and begin to feel part of the group. It's an exciting process with a lot of potential for ensuring a pleasant and productive school year.

Many kindergarten teachers start off the year with a theme of some kind, and plan activities within that theme. Some teachers choose to start the academic curriculum from Day One, focusing on skills such as learning the alphabet and counting. Other kindergarten teachers believe the academics can wait while the focus is put on the social curriculum.

67

> When children enter kindergarten, they should discover that each class is a working, problem-solving unit and that each student has both individual and group responsibilities.
>
> —William Glasser

The social curriculum is a good place to start because there are many skills children need to acquire prior to learning academic skills and concepts. If your students aren't sure how to listen in a group, don't know where to find supplies, or haven't a clue about finding a chair at a table, they will have many difficulties functioning in a group, completing their work, and being happy, productive members of the class.

It is wise to avoid making assumptions about your students. They should be shown how to do just about everything, from raising their hands to using a glue stick. You will have students who aren't sure how to sit in a circle and who have never had to wait in line at the drinking fountain. Some will only know how to grab for what they want, and some may wet their pants because they don't know where the restroom is. Invest the time now in helping your students function in the classroom and you'll reap the benefits throughout the year!

Start Slowly

Start off the year simply. Have a small selection of materials available and open up the learning centers gradually.

Use the "Mystery Bag"

Use your meeting times on the rug to introduce materials. You can heighten interest by hiding them in a "mystery bag." Ask the children for their ideas on how to use the materials. Limit the lessons to one or two items each time. Try a marker and a pencil, a paper towel and soap, or scissors and construction paper.

Introduce Learning Centers

Show small groups of students how to use each learning center, including where to find supplies and how to clean up. Discuss ways to share the space and materials. Spend a few weeks rotating everyone through the centers. Some teachers have students earn "licenses." These are cards that list each learning center. Students wear them on strings, and a hole is punched in the appropriate space each time a child completes the introduction to a learning center.

Set Expectations

Help children learn how to sit and listen in a group, and how to take turns sharing ideas and materials. Use role modeling and discussion. Point out specific examples of desired behavior. For example, "I can tell Maria is paying attention. Her body is still and her eyes are looking at me" is more specific than, "I like how Maria is sitting" or "Wonderful job, Maria."

Maintain a slow, gentle pace and a positive and reassuring manner.

CREATING A CARING CLASSROOM

All teachers want a happy classroom. A happy classroom is one in which the children feel physically and emotionally safe and secure. It is a place where the children have a sense of belonging to a group of people that cares for them. A caring classroom is one in which every child is valued, individual differences are accepted, and basic human rights are respected. The children show they care for one another by listening to each other, cooperating together, and helping each other. One way to create a caring classroom is by having a morning meeting.

Morning Meeting

The Morning Meeting is an excellent way to start the day. When the children sit in a circle on the rug, they immediately feel connected to the group. They can sing songs, play games, and share stories. With your gentle and sensitive guidance, your students can build a climate of trust and support during this time. Later in the year, the Morning Meeting is also a good time for focusing on academic skills. Some excellent activities for community building include:

Friendly greetings—Sing welcome songs, show children how to shake hands, using eye contact and saying each other's names.

Sharing—Also called "news" or "show and tell," this is an activity where a few students each day tell about something special or bring in an item to show the group. Children are encouraged to bring treasures from nature or favorite books instead of commercial toys. They can choose other students to ask them questions. In the interest of time, you will need to limit the number of "sharers" and questions per session.

Games—Fun, non-competitive circle games will get everyone involved and maybe even laughing! Include cooperative games that foster interdependence.

Also play name games and other activities which involve children in learning about each other or affirming how much they know. ("I'm thinking of someone who has an 'f' in her name, and she loves to build tall towers.")

Singing—Always sing in your meetings. Include songs which incorporate students' names, ideas, clothing, and favorite foods in their lyrics.

Problem-solving—Help the children work together to come up with ideas and solutions, whether it's deciding how to include others in recess play or what project to create in the block area. Children having problems with others can also get help at this time. Write down their ideas.

Create Class Rules

Other ways to create a caring community include involving the children in the creation of classroom rules. Teaching and enforcing "The Golden Rule" is a good way to introduce students to the general concept of respect for others.

Complete Group Projects

Consider establishing a group identity by giving the class a name and by including some whole-class, cooperative projects such as putting on a play, collecting coats for others, or making soup for a homeless shelter. Fund-raising by selling something students made or constructing something together, like a space ship or time machine, are also community-building activities.

Check It Out!

Positive Discipline in the Classroom by Jane Nelson, Lynn Lott, and H. Stephen Glenn (Prima Publishing, 1993).

Resources from *The Responsive Classroom* series, published by the Northeast Foundation for Children, 71 Montague City Road, Greenfield, MA 01301.

Teaching Children to Care: Management in the Responsive Classroom by Ruth Sidney Charney (Northeast Foundation for Children, 1992).

The Peaceful Classroom by Charles A. Smith, Ph.D. (Gryphon House, 1993).

You Can't Say You Can't Play by Vivian Gussin Paley (Harvard University Press, 1992).

Recognize Good Behavior

Reinforce positive social behavior throughout the day by acknowledging positive actions when you see them. ("I noticed you let Ming have the glitter, which was very helpful" or "I see you have really learned how to walk safely with those scissors.")

Set up a "peace watch" in which children report evidence of peaceful or caring behavior, such as "Leon helped me pick up the crayons Maya dropped" or "Sally and Antonio used words to work out their problem." These reportings are written on a big chart and shared daily. Some teachers have a "peace tree" and the children put up peace leaves with the words on them.

Redirect Undesirable Behavior

When encountering undesirable behavior, you may choose to ignore it. This may work for whining, tattling, and talking out of turn. Of course, you should stop behavior immediately if it's unsafe or hurtful.

You might redirect undesirable behaviors by offering alternatives. "Tables aren't for climbing. You may climb on this ladder instead."

In any case, look for the motive behind the behavior and see if you can support the child in getting his or her needs met in more constructive ways. Guide the child through the process of understanding why a behavior is unacceptable and coming up with alternative behavior.

DEALING WITH DIFFICULT BEHAVIOR

Year in and year out, most teachers confront some kinds of behavior problems in their classrooms. The difficulties you encounter will be as many and varied as the reasons for the problems. Some problems will be in your control and, sadly, some won't. The best thing to do is to try to prevent problems from arising in the first place. Some ways of doing this are listed below.

Be Clear

Have clear expectations for the children. These need to be reviewed and reinforced frequently with young children. Keep the rules simple, and state them as positively as possible.

Be Realistic

Make sure your expectations are developmentally appropriate. If you expect five-year-olds to sit still for 40 minutes, act "perfect," or not play or eat for several hours, you will have behavior problems!

Reinforce Positive Behavior

Model the behavior you want to see in the children. If you are calm, respectful, friendly, and giving, your students will be more inclined to act that way, too. Pay attention to positive behavior. Reinforce it with smiles, touches, and words.

> As you look at your youngsters, be sure that your standards of promptness, of attention, of quiet, of courtesy, are realistically geared to children, not idealistically geared to angels.
>
> —James L. Hymes, Jr., "The Oldest Order Changeth," NEA Journal, April 1953

Pay Attention

Observe your students carefully. Are their intellectual, physical, and social needs being met? Do you notice any changes in a child? Has a parent informed you of something that could lead to problem behavior (new medication, death of a grandparent, divorce, new baby, etc.)?

If behavior problems do arise, try not to panic or get upset. If a child is disruptive, calmly let the child know what is expected. If the problem persists, remind them of the consequences. ("If you keep jumping up during story time, I will ask you to go sit at a table until you're ready to be here with us.") Try to avoid "public" humiliation by talking to the child as privately as possible. Let them know you trust them to succeed. ("I know you're ready to walk in line now. You'll do great!")

Look Deeper

Think about what might be causing the problem. If you're lucky enough to have a classroom assistant, discuss your concerns with him or her. What is the child trying to get from the misbehavior? When did the problem behavior start? Have you noticed a pattern to it? Keeping notes can be very helpful. You may discover that something as unusual as an environmental or food sensitivity could be the cause.

Question Your Approach

How has your response to this behavior helped or hindered progress with this child? What are some alternate strategies?

Ask for Help

Elicit help from others. Let the parents know your concerns and ask for their ideas and support. (Be as positive and professional as possible so parents won't feel too upset or defensive.) Your principal, guidance counselor, and other teachers may also help.

Listen

Talk to the child who is having difficulties. Practice reflective listening without judgments and lectures. ("You are really upset that Carlos hasn't been playing with you," instead of "Of course Carlos isn't playing with you! You don't play fair.") After you have the child's trust, you can guide him or her through the process of changing the problem behavior.

Facilitate Communication

Help the children learn how to work out their problems with each other. Five-year-olds can learn to listen to each other and come up with solutions. This can be modeled in a group setting too, such as a class meeting.

> **When you're dealing with a child, keep all your wits about you, and sit on the floor.**
>
> —Austin O'Malley

Recognize and Reinforce Desired Behavior

Reinforce the desired behavior when it happens. A "happy note" (see page 91) put in a backpack brings a proud smile to a child's face. Be cautious about using other rewards for good behavior, such as candy or stickers. Children can get confused about what the real purpose of behaving is.

Use Time-outs.

Use time-outs when a child needs a few minutes to cool off or think about his or her behavior. Time-outs are most effective when they're brief and carried out calmly. If you're giving time-outs every day to the same child, you may need to evaluate their effectiveness.

Offer Alternatives

Children can let off steam by exercising, pounding clay, singing loudly, laughing, dancing and jumping to music, or going outside to run and scream. Calming activities include rocking, stretching to soothing music, or getting a back-rub. Sensory experiences, such as stroking the class pet, playing in water, finger painting, and smelling fragrances can also be relaxing.

Keep Your Cool

Finally, remember that even the best teachers can get angry sometimes. When this happens, try to back off for a bit, take some deep breaths and ask someone else to take over for a few minutes. You could even tell the child, "This is really upsetting me now, and in a little while we will talk about it." Monitor your feelings so you don't lose control!

CLASSROOM MANAGEMENT TIPS

Learning how to organize activities and students so that things run smoothly throughout the day can be one of the biggest challenges for teachers. Even veteran teachers look for ways to manage their programs more effectively! Here are some suggestions that may help you get off to a good start.

Keep It Simple

Avoid having lots of activities, clutter, and excessive noise. Too many dumped tubs of toys and students yelling for help will create chaos.

Have a clean, organized room. Signs and labels on materials and shelves will help the children know where to put things away properly. Modeling how and where to put things is also important.

Have an established place where students put their personal items as soon as they enter the classroom. They will need daily reminders to check their backpacks for notes from home.

Position yourself in the room so that you can see everyone.

Recruit Helpers

Enlist the children's help with attendance, milk count, or distributing papers. Kindergartners love to help!

Have Clear Expectations

Explain ahead of time how the space and materials will be used during an activity.

Give children enough time to complete their work and play.

Make sure children know where to put finished and unfinished projects and what to do when they're done with an activity.

If things get out of hand (the noise level is too high, messes are being left, children are running), call everybody over to the rug. Relax, review your expectations, discuss the problem, and try again.

Use Signals

Give children a five-minute warning before clean-up time. Ring a bell, sing a song, and make sure everyone hears you.

Use a special signal to signify "freezing" or "listening," such as ringing a bell or darkening the room. Use a whisper or singing voice to capture the children's attention.

Plan Learning Centers

Use a "choice board" with pictures to help the children know where they can go during work or choice time. They can put their names on their choices of learning centers. You may need to limit the number of children who can be in each of the centers. Center signs can indicate this. Popular stations can have timed periods and waiting lists for signing up.

Take Notes

Keep notes about where and how the children work and play, and who they tend to interact with. This will be helpful in planning activities, assessing development, and encouraging children to try new experiences.

Utilize Volunteers

Use your assistant and volunteers wisely by having them actively involved with the children as much as possible. Or, volunteers can free you to work with students by preparing materials for you.

Group Students for Activities

Have a system for insuring that the children get to their "must-do's." Rotate groups through some activities, or put names on the choice board when you want certain students to participate in a particular activity. Some teachers put stars by the "must-do's," both on the choice board and at the activity itself. A class list is helpful at "must-do's," because children can cross out their names when done.

Consider dividing the class in half for certain activities. Perhaps half can go to library time while you keep the other half for writing workshop.

Plan Classroom Visits

Visit other kindergartens. Other teachers can be great resources for classroom management ideas!

> **Anyone can steer a ship when the sea is calm.**
>
> —Publilius Syrus

PREPARE FOR SUBSTITUTES

Substitute teachers have a difficult job, especially if they are unfamiliar with your class or your school. The more prepared you are for a substitute, the greater the chances that he or she will have a pleasant and productive day with your students.

If you know in advance that you will be away from your classroom, you will have an opportunity to write detailed plans for your substitute. If you have an assistant or experienced volunteer, you can ask that person to help the substitute. You can also ask your aide or volunteer to communicate any special instructions you might have.

There may be times when you are unexpectedly unable to go to school. One way to prepare for these days is to have a substitute folder. Keep your folder in a conspicuous place in your classroom. Your folder should contain the following:

- the substitute information sheet (page 92)

- a class list, including detailed information on which children have special needs (allergies, disabilities) and which receive special services (speech therapy, occupational therapy)

- basic schedules, both daily and weekly, that include recess, meals, and special classes

- any important information about classroom procedures such as snack, milk count, special jobs

- a schedule showing when other adults work in the room (aides, tutors, therapists, parent volunteers)

- a list of rules, including recess guidelines

- a map of the school, indicating where the gym, cafeteria, nurse's office, library, and other important places are. Emergency procedures, such as fire drill information, should also be included

- a map or list of where important supplies and equipment are stored

- activity suggestions

- tips for classroom management

ASSESSMENT

Assessment—observing, testing, documenting, and evaluating the growth and development of children—is a big topic these days. How teachers chart the progress of their students depends on the school they work in as well as how they view children and learning. Many schools are in a period of transition regarding assessment, as they wrestle with "authentic" assessment, checklists, portfolios, running records, writing samples, rubrics, developmental reading assessments, and more.

You will need to find out how your school expects you to assess your students. Sometimes there are clear guidelines to help you, other times you're left on your own. In any case, here are some suggestions regarding assessment in kindergarten.

> **It's not how smart are you, but how are you smart?**

Establish a System

Set up a file box for your records. Make a file for each student and keep your notes and work samples in them.

Document your students' work. This means taking daily notes about what they do, what they say, who they play with, and so on. Keep or photocopy samples of their drawings and writings, and photograph their projects when you can. Date everything.

Chart your students' progress over time. For example, have them do at least three "writing" samples during the year. A sample involves making a picture and "writing" about it.

Involve the children in selecting art or writing samples for their folders. Write down what they say about them.

Keep Student Journals.

Writing, math, and science journals can provide good information on the children's thinking. Add your own "notes and quotes" in cases where the children have difficulty writing or drawing. This will give a more realistic view of their thinking.

Record Group Discussions

Enlist the help of your aide or other adult for documenting student work. In other words, if you and the children are on the rug discussing nighttime, their comments can be written down by your helper.

Show Off Student Work

Display some of your documentation. Their science predictions, math estimates, field trip comments, and drawings can all be put up in the classroom. Save what you can, as they will be useful during evaluation and reporting time.

Use Observations

Unless your school requires otherwise, you may not need to do much in the way of formal testing. Most of what you need to know you can see in the work of the children as they're involved in their daily activities. Through careful observation you can see who can zip a jacket, write his or her name, and tell you that "music" begins with "m."

If you need particular information on a child, try to elicit it by his or her participation in an activity. For example, you can assess knowledge of letters through playing alphabet bingo, and can watch jumping by inviting students to jump rope at recess.

Stay Relaxed

Sometimes more formal assessments are required. If you do need to use a particular instrument for record-keeping purposes, maintain a low-key, positive attitude during the "test," as some children get nervous in these situations.

Avoid getting caught up in excessive record-keeping. If you're spending more time with notebooks, charts, clipboards, and sticky notes than you are with children, it's time to assess yourself and the whole assessment process!

REPORTING

How and when we report our students' progress varies from school to school. Most schools have some kind of report card or progress report on which teachers write comments regarding their students' growth and development in the different learning domains. Report cards vary in their appropriateness for kindergarten. Some contain long checklists of skills and concepts as a basis for summarizing and reporting student progress. There is great variability in the language accompanying these checklists, ranging from "unsatisfactory" and "needs improvement" to the more positive "not yet" or "needs more time." Some report cards are more narrative, allowing the teacher to write entire paragraphs about each child.

Other schools don't issue progress reports but instead keep portfolios on each child. A portfolio is a collection of the child's work that is shared with the parents at conference time. Some of the portfolio contents are kept by the school and passed on to the next grade. Some schools use a combination of reporting methods. You'll need to find out early on what is expected from you regarding assessment and reporting.

Tips for Successful Reporting

Be Positive

Make your comments as positive as possible. Parents can feel very vulnerable when it comes to statements about their children. Don't avoid saying what needs to be said. You want to paint an honest picture of the child, but phrase your words carefully. One way to do this is to describe the behavior that concerns you, instead of giving it a label. For example, "Taylor sometimes knocks others' blocks down when she wants a turn in the block center" is more effective than "Taylor is aggressive with others." It gives the parent a clearer picture and avoids a label that can be upsetting.

Include children's strengths and interests. It's always good to focus on what the children do well, and to mention what they particularly enjoy. Parents appreciate hearing good news from teachers and like to feel you know their child.

Be Clear

Give examples of the child's learning. "Roberto is making progress with his literacy development." is much less specific than "Roberto joins with others in shared reading experiences, can predict words in books, and uses the first and last letters in words as he writes (*PL* for *pool*)."

Be Complete

Cover all areas of growth and development. Remember social growth, music, science, P.E., and all areas of the kindergarten program. Be sure to get input from all the other teachers who work with the children.

Be Creative

Adapt the report card. If you're not comfortable with your school's report card, ask your principal if you can include a page of your own comments for the parents. He or she may want to read them before they're sent home.

CHAPTER 4: RELATIONSHIPS

RELATIONSHIPS WITH YOUR SCHOOL STAFF

Along with creating a caring classroom and fostering good relationships with your students, it is essential that you develop a good rapport with school staff and the parents of your students. This isn't always easy, especially if you are in a large school or feel too busy to be sociable. But do take the time to connect with others in your building. You'll be more comfortable when you feel you're a part of things. Furthermore, some of the school staff will be instrumental in helping you succeed in your new job.

Your Aide (Paraprofessional)

Your aide is your teammate. Together you create the learning environment for your students. Good communication is vital, so make time to talk and plan with your aide on a regular basis. Classroom assistants vary in their experience and abilities, and it's better to utilize them where their strengths and interests lie. Find out what your aide feels comfortable doing and what training he or she will need. Keep communication open, and let your aide know how much his or her work is appreciated!

77

> **It is better to ask some of the questions than to know all of the answers.**
>
> —James Thurber, <u>The James Thurber Carnival</u>

Your Co-Teacher

You may be in a team-teaching situation, or share a classroom with another teacher. This situation is always easier when you are compatible in philosophy and style. If not, come to agreement about the room setup, curriculum, and teaching approaches. Perhaps you can take turns (by month or semester) with how centers are set up. Be flexible. If there are real difficulties, see if your principal can help. Above all, keep a positive attitude and your sense of humor!

Your Grade-Level Teachers

Kindergarten teachers can sometimes feel isolated from other teachers in their school because they have different schedules and may have classrooms in separate areas of the school. If there are other teachers in your school who teach kindergarten, consider yourself very lucky. They can be a tremendous support system for you, whether by sharing materials or giving helpful advice. Take time to know these teachers. They can become true friends.

Take some time before school opens to make the rounds of your new school. Stop into the classrooms and introduce yourself to the other teachers. Try to remember their names. You'll be interacting with them in staff and committee meetings, on the playground and at other school events, so it's good for you to know one another.

The "Specials" Teachers

If there are teachers who take your students for art, music, and physical education, meet them too. Ask these teachers how you can prepare your students for "specials" time. They will really appreciate it. Ask if it's okay to occasionally see how your students are doing in the class. Have them notify you if they have any concerns about any of your students. Keep communication going throughout the year!

The Special Education Staff

If you have students requiring special education (SPED) services, it is important to have good relationships with the therapists who will be providing the services. You may be working with a speech and language pathologist, an occupational therapist, a physical therapist, a resource room teacher, and maybe even a "one-to-one aide" if you have a student requiring full-time assistance. You'll need to meet with these people to discuss schedules, goals, classroom modifications, and activities. Finding the time to coordinate therapy sessions and consultation meetings can be a challenge. Again, be as flexible and positive as possible. Find out from your principal what the policies and procedures are for the SPED program, what your duties are, and how and where records are to be kept.

The Guidance Counselor

As someone who can give you help with a troubled student or even visit your classroom to lead a discussion, the guidance counselor can be a real asset to your program. He or she can speak to your students or direct activities about personal and social issues.

The School or District Psychologist

Your school or district psychologist may not be on campus full-time, but when he or she comes around, introduce yourself. You may be working with the psychologist if there are serious emotional, behavioral, or cognitive concerns about a student, or when educational testing is involved.

The Nurse

School nurses play a significant role in the lives of kindergartners, for they test vision and hearing, and they are at the ready to comfort sore tummies, put ice on bumped heads, and bandages on scraped knees. Get to know your school nurse, and find out everything you can about policies and procedures regarding first aid, sickness, and emergencies. Ask if he or she is interested in helping with any of your health education activities.

The Librarian

A good librarian is a gold mine, and can help you in numerous ways. Librarians may read stories to your class and help your students check out books. They can also help you find materials. The best librarians want to know what you're teaching so they can find resources for you. They are often the school media technology experts as well. Return borrowed materials on time!

The Cooks

A good relationship with the school cooks is important for many reasons. Your students may have breakfast or lunch provided by the school, and you want it to be a pleasant experience for everyone. Find out from the cooks what they expect from you and your students, then help out as much as you can. If you purchase milk from the kitchen, keep good records and hand in the money on time. Cooks may also let you use the oven for class projects and occasionally lend you supplies.

The Bus Drivers

The people who transport your students to and from school have a very important job. Some friendly recognition on your part will go a long way. Introduce yourself to the bus drivers, and ask them if there's anything you and your students can do to make their jobs easier. Be sure your students know how to be safe and respectful on the bus. Kindergartners often do best sitting in the front of the bus. Keep in touch with the driver about any problems.

The Secretary

The school secretary's job is so important that teachers often joke that it's the secretary who really runs the school! There's a lot of truth in this, for it's the secretary who greets visitors, sees the students who come to the office, answers the telephone, types the letters, and orders the supplies. Both staff and students rely on the secretary for many things, as he or she is often the one holding down the fort while the principal attends meetings. Be very nice to your secretary by returning forms on time and not burdening him or her with too many questions and favors.

We are going to have to find ways of organizing ourselves cooperatively, sanely, scientifically, harmonically and in regenerative spontaneity with the rest of humanity around earth . . .

We are not going to be able to operate our spaceship earth successfully nor for much longer unless we see it as a whole spaceship and our fate as common. It has to be everybody or nobody.

—Buckminster Fuller

The Custodian

Along with the secretary, the custodian reigns supreme in the eyes of teachers. A friendly and competent custodian is a blessing, for you will need his or her help throughout the year. Custodians can find you furniture, assemble an easel, repair equipment, and wipe up emergency spills of an unpleasant nature. Be kind to your custodian by maintaining your room and by understanding that he or she is very busy and can't always be at your beck and call.

The Principal and Vice-Principal

All teachers want a good relationship with their principals, as it can make a big difference in how they feel about their jobs. Principals vary in their administrative style; some visit classrooms and show an interest in how and what's being taught, while others maintain a distance. Try to develop a good rapport with your principal by being respectful, professional, and enthusiastic about your job. Be positive in the face of difficult circumstances, flexible during decision-making, and patient if it's taking a while to get what you need. Principals have stressful jobs and they appreciate teachers who are supportive. If your principal likes and appreciates you, your job will be much easier! Furthermore, if problems do occur, your principal will be more open to resolving any conflicts if a good relationship has already been established.

Building Relationships at Your School

1. Sit with other staff members at lunch or during breaks, even if you're busy and not feeling sociable. It'll help you feel part of the school "family."

2. Ask for teaching advice. Those who want to help will be very pleased to talk to you about their ideas.

3. Help out as much as you can. Donate money to the "sunshine fund," volunteer at a fund-raiser, serve on a committee.

4. Show your appreciation to all who help you and your students by giving cards and little gifts. Custodians, bus drivers, and cooks are among the many who deserve more recognition!

5. Be on time for everything.

6. Be a good listener.

7. Try not to be negative or critical, and avoid gossip.

8. Dress attractively. Kindergarten teachers shouldn't be expected to wear high heels and suits, but you can look professional in slacks and comfortable shoes.

9. Be friendly, positive, and sincere.

10. Smile!

PARENTS ARE YOUR GREATEST ALLIES!

Your students' parents can also have a tremendous influence on how you feel about your job. When they are trusting and friendly toward you, it makes it a lot easier to teach their children. When they show an interest in your program and offer to help out, it is a wonderful feeling. With luck, you will have parents who show up for open house, remember the milk money, and communicate with you if they have any questions or concerns. The reality is that there may be a parent who creates difficulties at some point. When you have an uncomfortable relationship with a parent it's easy to let it dampen your spirits.

Fortunately, most parents feel positive toward kindergarten teachers, especially when they see their little ones so happy to go to school! You can greatly increase your chances of developing positive relationships with the parents of your students by remembering the following points.

Involve

Parents are your allies. They, like you, want what's best for the child. Approach parents as fellow team members in educating and caring for their children.

Some parents may want an opportunity to participate in your program. Perhaps they can chaperone a field trip, send in a special snack, or help out in the classroom.

Reassure

Some parents need a lot of reassurance about their children. Taking the extra time to allay their worries is a worthy investment.

Most parents want to know how great their kids are doing. Don't wait for a problem to occur before calling a parent.

> I never before understood the depth of gratitude a parent can feel for a teacher who creates a classroom environment that enables children to love learning, to exhibit genuine enthusiasm and excitement for purposeful and meaningful tasks, and to experience a feeling of belonging to a new community of friends.
>
> —Irene Hannigan, Off to School—A Parent's-Eye View of the Kindergarten Year (NAEYC, 1998)

Respect

Not all families are the same. Be aware of and respect the cultural and religious views of the families. For example, don't assume all your students eat meat and celebrate Christmas.

Communicate

Probably 90% of difficulties teachers and parents have are due to lack of communication. Schedule a parent orientation well before school starts (in the late spring or summer). If your school doesn't have one, plan your own Back to School Night or Open House in the fall. Meeting with them face-to-face helps establish a relationship early on. Send home regular classroom newsletters so that parents know what's going on. (Use the reproducible on page 93.)

Be warm and welcoming toward the parents. Be relaxed and be yourself while remaining the professional you are. Of course you want them to like you, but you especially want them to trust you. Having the support of parents can give you a real lift throughout the year!

Have a Positive Parent Conference!

Involve Parents

Include the parents in making their own appointments. Ask for their time and day preferences. You can post a sign-up sheet at Open House.

Mail parents invitations/confirmations of their conference time. Provide them with a means to respond and reschedule, if needed.

Prior to the conference, send home a letter saying how much you're looking forward to meeting them, and asking them to think about what kinds of things they would like to know about your program and their child's progress. Suggest that they ask their child for three questions for you to answer!

If the parents don't speak English, find out ahead of time if they will need an interpreter.

Provide a Welcoming Environment

Have a comfortable waiting area for the parents. Provide parenting books, class books, and other items of interest for them to look at. You might even provide pattern blocks to play with!

Keep to your scheduled time so parents don't have to wait too long.

Be warm and welcoming, shake hands, and thank them for coming.

Be sure everyone sits equally. In other words, avoid sitting behind a desk or in a teacher chair while parents sit in children's chairs.

Have examples of the child's work and be sure your report is organized. Consider having some of the child's work available for the parents to take home.

Communicate Honestly

Start off positive. End on a positive note as well. Be honest about any concerns, but frame them in ways that make it easier for parents to hear and understand.

Include reports from other people who work with the child. If necessary, send your colleagues a form to complete and return to you prior to the conference.

Involve the parents in setting goals for their child. Their input is valuable and they need to know you regard them as partners in the education of their child. Ask them what they want their child to get from kindergarten and how you can help.

Be a good listener. Give parents your full attention.

Avoid Problems

Don't get defensive. When faced with criticism or hostility, listen and thank them for their comments.

Schedule another appointment if there are unresolved issues.

If you anticipate a problem with a parent, ask your principal to join your meeting. Notify the parent in advance.

Parent Involvement

It is a lucky teacher who has parent volunteers, and parents who want to help feel fortunate to be welcomed by the teacher.

Parent participation varies from school to school. Some teachers get so many helpers they have to rotate them to avoid having too many adults in the room. Other teachers can't find any parents to help out. Often parents want to help, but can't because of their jobs or because of younger siblings in the home. Sometimes parents feel too shy about volunteering, or lack the confidence to work in a classroom setting. For some, there are language and cultural barriers which make them uncomfortable about approaching you.

Some Ways Parents Can Help

Working With Students
Volunteers can assist children with art and other projects, read stories, play games and do puzzles, cook, or share a special story or activity from their work, family, or culture.

Preparing Materials
Parents can assist you by stapling, laminating, or photocopying papers. They can also type and bind students' books (which can be done at home), clean paint cups, hang bulletin boards, and prepare art project materials.

Volunteers can help at home by cutting out pattern shapes, laundering paint smocks, sewing and mending, or repairing toys.

Providing Supplies
Parents can shop for or donate snack foods, class materials, and other items.

Sharing Special Talents
Ask your parent volunteers *how* they would like to help. Parents can have many talents, and have been known to do magic shows, teach songs, lead hikes, bring fire trucks to school, and give slide shows on volcanoes. Even grandparents can get involved!

Encourage Parent Involvement

- Send home a letter explaining how you value parent help. As with other letters home, make sure it is in the language of the parents.

- List ways that parents can help you and ask if they are interested in helping. This could be a volunteer form that they return.

- Ask what times and days they are available.

- Be sure to thank them for their response and work out a volunteer schedule with them.

- Remember that many parents are busy and may not be able to help very often, if at all. They need to know that you understand this.

- Find ways that parents can help at home, if that's their preference.

- Orient classroom volunteers to the room before they begin, and explain how the activities are structured. Type guidelines for them.

- If a parent has difficulty with the children, perhaps he or she can help you with preparing materials and other tasks.

- Be sure you and the students are warm and welcoming to the parents, and address them the way they prefer.

- Show your appreciation to your volunteers through thank-you notes, little gifts, and maybe even a volunteer recognition lunch.

> There is a destiny that makes us brothers, none goes his way alone.
>
> All that we send into the lives of others comes back into our own.
>
> —Edwin Markham

CHAPTER FIVE: CLOSING THOUGHTS

HELPING CHILDREN WITH SPECIAL NEEDS

Overview

Teacher-training programs vary in the extent to which they prepare prospective regular education teachers for working with children who have special needs. If you are new to teaching or know little about learning disorders and other areas in which your students may require special services, it's a good idea to become informed. The federal government has reported that up to 12% of students in every classroom may have disabilities that need to be addressed. You may have students entering your program already on an Individualized Education Plan (I.E.P.), and you'll need to read the plan, understand it, and talk with the people who will be providing the services.

The most common disabilities that appear in kindergarten are speech and language delays and motor problems. However, you may also have students with autism, Attention Deficit Disorder (ADD), Attention Deficit Hyperactive Disorder (ADHD), as well as students with hearing and vision impairments, or those who are in wheelchairs or have severe physical or mental disabilities. One of your jobs as a teacher is to be aware of developmental delays or other problems appearing in your students.

> **We have one simple rule here: Be kind.**
>
> —Sam Jaffe, <u>Lost Horizon</u>, 1937

Signs to Watch For

- very young speech, or "baby talk"

- speech that is difficult to understand

- frequently asking "What?"; not hearing or understanding others

- gross motor difficulties—clumsy, awkward movements or poor balance

- small motor difficulties—trouble holding pencil, scissors

- confused by directions, trouble remembering

- work and self-care tasks below chronological-age level

- excessively active, noisy, impulsive, or excitable behaviors

Many times the behavior that concerns you may change as the child matures and becomes accustomed to the classroom. Often we think something is wrong with a child, when he or she is simply developing at a different (but normal) rate. In some cases it's a matter of experience, as some children have had limited exposure to crayons and scissors prior to kindergarten. It's best not to be alarmed. Instead, talk to someone in your school who can help, such as your special education teacher or principal.

Kindergarten Screening

Sometimes there is a real cause for concern, and early intervention can help. Federal law requires that every public school submit a plan for identifying and supporting students with disabilities. One way that schools ensure that children get the help they need is to screen every kindergarten child. If you teach in a public school, it is likely your students were screened in the spring (or possibly in the summer), or that they will be tested in the fall after they've started their kindergarten year. You may have a part in the screening. This is advisable, as your students will be comfortable with you and you can learn more about them. Other teachers, district personnel, or contracted screeners from outside the district may also be involved. Generally, your students are tested in the areas of basic concepts, speech and language, and large and small motor skills. They will receive a vision and hearing screening as well.

Evaluation

Once the screening results are reviewed and discussed, decisions are made about which children may need monitoring and which may need to be rescreened. Children who show a potential weakness in an area are often recommended for an evaluation, which is usually done by the therapist in that area of concern (speech therapist, occupational or physical therapist). The child may have to leave the classroom several times to complete the evaluation. Sometimes teachers work together to have the evaluation take place in the classroom or on the playground if a child is uncomfortable with being "pulled" from the class. Parental permission is required for an evaluation, and concerned teachers or parents can request an evaluation at any time during the year.

Team Meetings

Sometimes called a "core," team meetings are where the teachers, therapists, and parents come together to discuss the results of an evaluation, plan goals for the child, or review and update an I.E.P. An administrator (or someone representing him or her) needs to be in attendance as well. You will most likely be called upon to describe the child's progress and explain what you've been doing to meet the child's needs. An example or two of the child's work is helpful.

Services

Once an I.E.P. (or other similarly designated plan) is in place, children must start receiving special services. Talk to your principal and special education staff about what is expected of you and the therapists involved. Some students may require only a modification to your program and will not need additional services.

The ways in which SPED and support services are provided vary from school to school, and even from teacher to teacher. Some therapists follow a pull-out model, and will usually come and pick up students from your classroom. Others use an inclusion model and will provide services in your classroom. This latter approach, sometimes called mainstreaming, is favored by many teachers because it prevents the SPED students from feeling singled out, or that they're missing out on all the fun in their classrooms. Another advantage is that the therapist can incorporate the lesson within your classroom, sometimes even leading a whole-group activity or facilitating at one of the learning centers while other students serve as models for the desired behaviors. Furthermore, you can learn a great deal about how to help your students by watching the therapists at work!

> There are only two lasting bequests we can hope to give our children. One of these is roots; the other, wings.
>
> —Hodding Carter

Ways You Can Help Your Special Education Students

- Meet regularly with the therapists. You can plan activities together, share strategies, and learn a lot from each other about how to help these children on an ongoing basis. For example, to support children who need to practice articulating certain sounds, you can play games or lead chants and songs that include those sounds. Children with large muscle weaknesses may need to sit in a different way at circle times (on a ball or bean bag chair, for example). Students who have auditory processing problems may benefit from sitting where there are the fewest distractions. Restless and distractable students may need to sit next to the teacher, where his or her hand can calm them.

- Communicate regularly with parents about student progress. Provide them with activities for helping at home. The therapists can help with this.

- Think of ways you can modify your teaching or change the environment to help students with special needs. Consult your special education teacher and therapists for ideas.

- Realize that some of these children may lack confidence and will need encouragement, patience, and many opportunities to work hard and succeed!

ENGLISH LANGUAGE DEVELOPMENT

Helping Non-English Speaking Students

We have always been a nation of immigrants, and large numbers of families continue to come to the United States from around the world. Many children enter schools having spoken little or no English. Today's classrooms and playgrounds are filled with the sounds of Spanish, Chinese, Khmer, Vietnamese, and many other world languages. These students need a lot of support from teachers in order to feel comfortable in school and to learn successfully.

Because you teach kindergarten, you are most likely the first formal teacher these children will encounter. You may also be the first adult they've met who doesn't speak their language. These children may be anxious and confused. They may have difficulty understanding what is being said and trouble communicating their own thoughts to others. There may also be cultural differences that lead to confusion and misunderstandings.

These students will need your reassuring smiles and gentle guidance. A lot can be understood through body language and pictures, and with the help of the entire classroom community, these children can begin to feel safe, secure, and competent. Here are some ways to help your non-English speakers.

Ask for Help

Enlist the help of ESL or English Language Development teachers, as well as any bilingual teachers on staff, especially those who may work with your students. If there are several students in your classroom who speak the same language, talk to your principal about the possibility of having a tutor who can translate and introduce new concepts in the children's native language.

Build English Vocabulary

Help these students begin to learn English. If a child is the only person in the classroom who speaks a particular language, he or she will learn English much more quickly. However, if there are others who share the same language, the children can help each other communicate and feel comfortable. Fortunately, kindergarten activities are very conducive to learning English, because of the focus on language development. Reading predictable texts, chanting, singing with hand motions, shared reading, and movement activities are just some of the ways that children can learn English.

Try New Approaches

Help students understand what is being said by adding hand motions and other gestures, acting words out (modeling), and showing or drawing pictures of what you mean. Also try explaining difficult concepts in several different ways. This will help not only second-language learners, but all the students in your classroom!

Check for Understanding

Always check for understanding. Don't assume children know everything you said about the playground rules or learning center directions.

Buddy Up

Pair students with English-speaking "buddies." This partnership will offer companionship. More importantly, it will give students an opportunity to communicate one-on-one.

Communicate

Be sure the notes you send home to the parents will be understood. You may need to find someone to translate important notes.

87

Learn New Things

Learn some of your students' native language. Ask students to help teach the class a few simple words. Everyone will enjoy learning phrases such as *please*, *thank you*, *hello*, and *good-bye*. Learn a simple poem or song, which will show your other students how challenging it can be to learn a second language!

THE ABUSED OR NEGLECTED CHILD

It is an unfortunate reality that some children come to school without breakfast or clean clothes, and maybe even after having been beaten by a parent or other household member. One of a teacher's most difficult and painful jobs is recognizing and reporting signs of abuse or neglect.

Signs of Abuse

Watch for signs of abuse or neglect. These include:

- being unkempt, dirty, tired, and hungry

- withdrawing from others

- being sullen or angry

- appearing anxious and nervous

- not wanting to go to home

- trouble sleeping

- appearing unusually fearful

- thumb sucking, nervous twitching, or tics

- frequent urination or feeling pain in genital area

- red marks, bruises, unexplained fractures and bumps

- child's stories, art, and behavior revealing knowledge of or preoccupation with violence, drinking, drugs, or sexual acts

Understand Your Responsibility

It is your legal obligation to report your suspicions about neglect or abuse. If you don't, you may be contributing to the pain and suffering of a child and can be held legally accountable. In some states you are required to report suspected child abuse to the police.

Alert your principal or guidance counselor immediately if you feel a child is being mistreated or is in danger of any kind.

Involve the guidance counselor in helping the child. It is his or her job to support students who may be abused or neglected.

Be Discreet

Keep you concerns confidential. Other teachers, parent volunteers, and school staff should not be informed of your suspicions. More importantly, if your suspicions turn out to be unfounded, the damage to reputations as well as to your parent relationships could be irreparable.

Communicate

Talk to the child calmly and privately. You may ask a few questions without putting the child on the spot, especially if you have a good rapport with the child and he or she seems willing to talk. A child who has been hurt may be too scared to tell you about it. If talking is distressing to the child, back off.

Be Reliable

Try to develop a trusting relationship with the child. You may be the only loving or reliable adult in his or her life.

Provide Outlets

Provide lots of opportunities for expression. Encourage the child to draw, paint, work with clay, tell you stories, and use the doll house. You may get a glimpse of the child's world through language and creations.

Every second we live is a new and unique moment of the universe, a moment that never was before and never will be again. And what do we teach our children in school? We teach them that two and two makes four and that Paris is the capital of France. When will we also teach them what they are? We should say to each of them: Do you know what you are? You are a marvel. You are unique. In all the world there is no other child exactly like you. In the millions of years that have passed there has never been a child like you. And look at your body. What a wonder it is! Your legs, your arms, your cunning fingers, the way you move! You may become a Shakespeare, a Michelangelo, a Beethoven. You have the capacity for anything. Yes, you are a marvel. And when you grow up can you then harm another who is, like you, a marvel? You must cherish one another. You must work—we must all work—to make this world worthy of its children.

—Pablo Casals

CLOSING WORDS

I recommend that you continue developing yourself as a teacher by attending workshops and conferences, taking courses at your local college or university, visiting other classrooms, finding a mentor teacher, and reading, reading, reading!

Take care of yourself. Teaching can be exhilarating and exhausting. Eat right, exercise, and get plenty of rest. Keep your life in balance, and you will be an effective teacher.

Be creative! Enjoy yourself! As I said in the introduction, every day is full of promise and possibilities. And most important of all, keep the child at the center of everything you do.

Joyful teaching to you!

I AM A V.I.P.!

My name is _____.

I am _____ years old.

I live at _____.

I live with _____.

I like to eat _____.

My favorite color is _____.

My favorite things to do are _____.

_____.

_____.

On the back of this paper is my drawing of

_____.

Today I plan to

_____

_____

_____

_____

_____

signed, _____

_____

Happy Note and Award Certificate

"Bee" very proud of _____

because _____

_____

I'm sure proud!

Sincerely,

_____

Substitute Information Sheet

Welcome to our class! You will find useful information in the substitute folder, including our class list, schedule, and important procedures.

Our daily activities are as follows:

Time   **Activity**

_____   _____

_____   _____

_____   _____

_____   _____

_____   _____

_____   _____

Emergency Procedures

The first aid kit can be found here: _____

If a child is sick or injured, please _____

_____

In case of fire, _____

_____

_____

In other emergency situations, please _____

_____

If you need any assistance, please contact _____ at _____

Thank you for coming to our class today. Please leave me a note telling me about your day. Also, please let me know if there is any additional information that may have been helpful to you, so that I can include it in the folder.

Kindergarten News

For the week of _____ Teacher _____

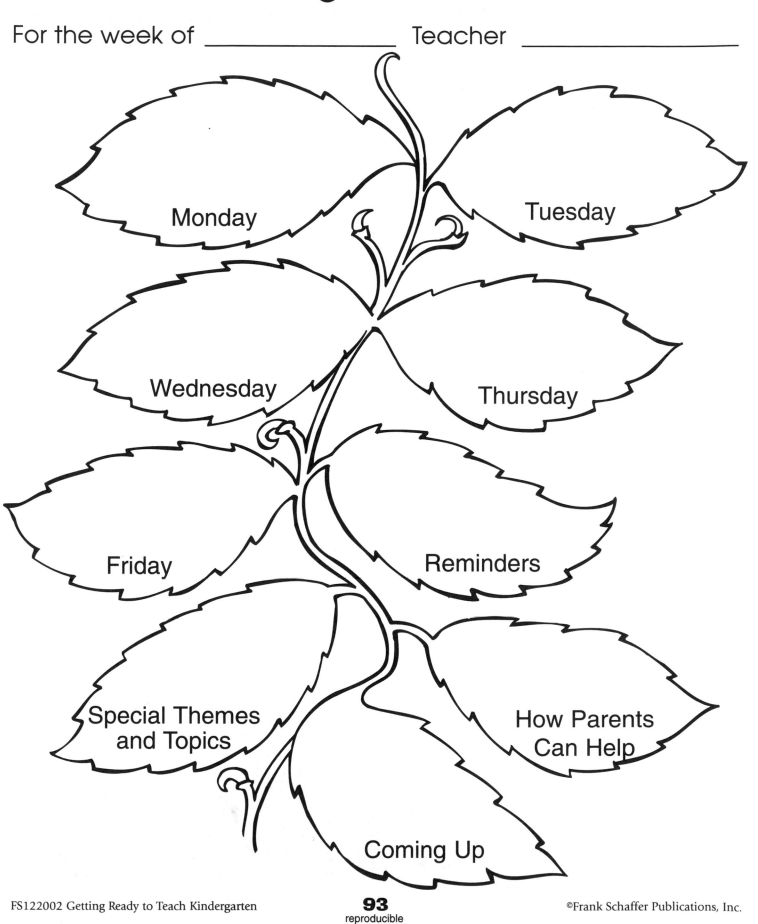

Monday

Tuesday

Wednesday

Thursday

Friday

Reminders

Special Themes and Topics

How Parents Can Help

Coming Up

CHILD INFORMATION QUESTIONNAIRE

Name of child _____ Birth date _____

Nickname or name to be used in school _____

Child lives with _____

Language(s) spoken in home _____

Previous day care or preschool experience? _____ If yes, please describe your child's experience.

_____

How does your child feel about starting kindergarten? _____

What do you hope your child will learn in kindergarten? _____

_____

What are your child's strengths and interests? _____

_____

Do you have any concerns we should know about, such as:

health concerns, allergies _____

learning or developmental problems _____

emotional concerns, such as fears and anxieties _____

How would you describe your child? _____

Is there anything else you would like us to know? _____

_____

Your name _____ Telephone _____

Relationship to child _____

Thank you for taking the time to provide us with the above information. It will help us a great deal in meeting the needs of your child. Please mail this form back to us or send it with your child on the first day of school.